News from Victo

Stanley Bernard

Paths publishing

Paths Publishing
2 The Compts, Peacehaven, East Sussex. BN10 7SQ
stanley3@btinternet.com

© 2014 Stanley Bernard

The right of Stanley Bernard to be identified as the Author of this work has been asserted in accordance with the Copyrights, Designs and Patents Act 1988.
All rights reserved. No part of this book may be reprinted or reproduced or utilised in any form or by electronic, mechanical or other means, now known or hereafter invented, including photocopying and recording, or in any information storage or retrieval system, without the permission in writing from the author.
British Library Cataloguing in publication Data.
A catalogue record for this book is available from the British Library
ISBN 978-0-95351867-8

Contents

Foreword.	1
Part 1. Population and employment.	
1. The time of the 1841 Census.	4
2. A developing town.	11
3. All Change by 1881.	24
Part 2. Victorian News.	
4. A New Queen.	33
5. All at Sea.	38
6. The new Lifeboat.	44
7. The flight of the King of France.	47
8. A riotous time.	50
9. Murder most horrid.	59
10. Other crimes or not!	73
References	84
Selected bibliography	89
Index	90

Acknowledgements

I would like to thank my wife for putting up with me disappearing for hours at a time to either a record office or my desk at home to work on this. Next, a big thank you to my tutors at the Open University for keeping me on track while completing my MA which has formed the basis of this book. Thanks must also go to the hard working staff at East Sussex Record Office for the help they gave. The late Tony Payne, then chairman of Peacehaven & Telscombe Historical Society, for letting me have his collection of slides, which have since been donated to the East Sussex Record Office. Also a big thank you to Newhaven Museum, without whose help there would not have been any of the old historical pictures of the town. Finally, for checking that this all makes sense and is readable, a thank you goes to Dani Carbery.

The copyright of the owners of the pictures is acknowledged with grateful thanks to, East Sussex Record Office (ESRO) now incorporated into The Keep, Newhaven Museum, The British Library and Illustrated London News (iln.org.uk). Every effort has been made to identify copyright holders. The publisher will be pleased to rectify any omissions in future reprints. All the photographs of Newhaven now, good and bad were taken by the author, unless otherwise stated.

About The Author.

Born in Edgware Middlesex, on his marriage moved to St Albans, before moving to Peacehaven with his wife and family in 1986.

Enrolling on the new Open University History MA course he choose as the subject of his dissertation Newhaven's housing and industrial development during the reign of Queen Victorian. Stanley was both surprised and pleased to be awarded a pass with Merit in 2012. It was this study that was the inspiration for this book. It is based on the historical facts plus all the interesting Victorian newspaper articles that were a wonderful distraction to academic study.

He has written a number of books on Peacehaven, including "Peacehaven & Telscombe Through Time" (Amberley Publishing 2009): Before the Bungalows & People of Telscombe and Peacehaven (Paths Publishing 2007 & 2003)

Foreword

What is about to be described here is not the town of Newhaven that we see today, which has declined following the closure of the docks and warehouses, but the Newhaven that saw itself as an up and coming major town with big ambitions. These ambitions were based on the advent of the railway in 1847 and the ferry services across the Channel and also to Jersey, which brought with them enhanced harbour and warehousing facilities to cater for the increase in cargo-carrying shipping.

During the early nineteenth century, visitors to Newhaven would have seen large houses, some with more than one big garden where, today, there are housing estates. Shops were built to provide goods for the ever growing population, where today they are now closed and boarded up. Employment opportunities were huge, attracting workers from all over the country, where now the Town Council struggles to persuade employers to come to the town.

The object of this book is to give an insight into the changes that had happened in Newhaven during the period when it changed from a small town and rural community into a major international port. From when Queen Victoria came to the throne in 1837 until her death at the beginning of the next century, England saw possibly the biggest series of changes in the lives of the inhabitants of virtually every town. Transport and technology brought about the massive transformations which meant that this Sussex town would grow to approximately six time its original size by 1900. Such a large increase over such a short space of time must have had a very marked effect on day to day life.

Newspapers in the Victorian period were just that; *news*papers. They may have had their own agendas, depending on the attitude of the editor, but they gave real news with little comment. We can also tell from how the articles were written how the readers were expected react to the reported events, although the readership consisted of mainly respectable people rather than common workers. Class was important and everyone knew or thought they knew how each sector of society should behave and so reacted accordingly. These newspapers make it possible to see what was happening in this small Sussex town which was, apparently, not always as jaded as we may think.

However, before looking at the news, it may be useful to see why a minority of locals and those passing through the town may have ended up in stories that were published both in the local and national press of the day. To do that, this first section looks at the changes in population and employment to help provide a background of Newhaven's growth and the effect this had on the working population.

At the beginning of this period, most people travelled on foot and walking many miles either to work or even just to buy a drink was normal. Working days were long and hard. However, when it came to crimes, their related punishments seem to be even harder to our modern eyes. It should be remembered that although life was hard at that time, it was what the ordinary person considered normal. It was their way of life and it is not really for us to condemn what we may see as cruel punishments a hundred years on.

How did the change in Newhaven's population and employment affect everyday life? Some things would not change. For example, being a coastal town ships often floundered, sometimes remarkably close to the safety of the harbour. There was found some noteworthy stories of bravery at sea as well as celebrations to commemorate the coming of a new lifeboat as well as the coronation of Queen Victoria.

However, a large population brings with it conflict and crime and, what seems to be a minor offence today may have been treated as a very serious misdemeanour in Victorian times. Standards and values were different and, even for the most serious of crimes, those who avoided the hangman's noose could face transportation or weeks of hard labour, together with solitary confinement, which was definitely not an easy option for those found guilty. These stories reflect all of this and more.

Included amongst the serious crimes of the day are just a few of the more frivolous stories in the papers. All of these give just a glimpse of life during this period.

Finally, on reading this book you will see a number of references to pubs, so here is a quote from the period which may well sum up the part they played in everyday life:-

"Here is another indication of the go-a-headedness of Newhaven. In consequence of the influx of the population, owing to the carrying out of the new harbour works, it has been though necessary to erect a new church. Accordingly, the Rector having presented for the purpose piece of glebe land, an iron building, with accommodation for seven hundred persons, will be erected, at the same number of pounds. Newhaven will be a big and important place yet, and during the progress of the town it may be noted that for every church opened several liquor shops will have sprung into existence. It is strange that wherever civilised Englishmen are to be met there will be found a place of worship and a public house. Of course I am not condemning the latter establishments, I am only noting what presents itself to my mind as a curious fact."[1]

The spelling of names is as they appear in the various publications used. This has led the author to wonder if some of those mentioned with similar names are the same persons. It is let to the reader to decide. The index has been complied by the author following editing and was not checked for accuracy, I apologise to the reader for error here or in any other part of this publication .

Part 1   Population and employment

Chapter 1.
The time of the 1841 Census.

When looking back at any area of the country, it is not only quite interesting but also often very useful as a starting point to look at the population in general terms and then to expand this information to include the type of work they did and also how many family members lived in one house. We can only really look at population records in detail from 1831 onwards, as this was the first census which was recorded this type of information and provides us with a useful a starting point. Even though there were census's carried out in 1801, 1811 and 1821, the information they provided was far too general and therefore of little use. In fact, in 1801, in the county of Sussex failed to complete its census as only a few parishes send back the basic information to complete their individual census returns.

Records show that, in 1831, the population of Newhaven consisted of fewer than one thousand people. They lived in a small mixed, urban, rural and maritime community. At the time there were only 211 houses recorded and, of these, four were listed as uninhabited.[2] This shows us that there were roughly four people living in each dwelling. There is no way of knowing what other types of accommodation people lived in at this time.

Moving forward half a century and using the same set of reports from the 1881 census, the population of Newhaven had grown to about four thousand persons who were now living in a much more urban community. Housing needs at this time were not well catered for, with many houses consisting of either more than one family or a family and a number of lodgers all living together. Although there were now around six hundred homes, with a further forty under construction, there could well have been much more overcrowding as there was now an average of 6 people in each dwelling. However, quite a few did not actually live in houses. According to this more recent census, there were quite a number of people living in huts, at addresses such as "seaside and works huts". These huts did not just house temporary navvies working on harbour improvements, as may be thought, but complete families. Such a growth in the population must have had a wide ranging impact on the trade and commerce of the town.

This dramatic change in population was highlighted in a report published in The Morning Post from December 1881. Although this particular report concentrated on the harbour, it describes the changes that had taken place over the previous thirty years. 'The railway traffic and shipping have attracted new inhabitants, and created a demand for houses, new shops, new wharves, which continue visibly on the increase, so as to occasion remark from periodical visitors. During the past five or six years about 200 houses have been added to the town.'3 As will be seen in the next chapter most of the construction of new housing in the town of Newhaven took place from the 1880's onwards.

This early picture shows a typical Newhaven shop, W D Stone was trading as both draper and grocer.

From the slide collection of The late Tony Payne

Those who were in business did so on a small scale, whether they were a local retailer or manufacturer. This was before 1847 when the railway came. Although there are always exceptions, it can be assumed that these business people were never rich and it was probably always a struggle for them to survive. Many would have been selling goods to the town's folk and those from surrounding villages. Looking at a local directory published just at the beginning of the period covered, it is possible to see how hard business was for some of the local traders. According to Pigot's directory for 1839, besides the two churches, there were two bakers, two butchers, five boot and shoemakers and seven grocers, most of whom combined their grocery trade with drapery.4 Other trades of note were the four inns or public houses, four coal merchants and two tailors. Like some other businessmen at the time, the stationers also combined their business with other employment, like John Hubard, who was also the school master while the other, George Smith was the registrar of births and deaths.

The nearby villages were, in essence, just small farming communities, and may well have relied on Newhaven for many of the goods they required. Even with this trade, as well as that from the town's residents, it was not always possible to earn a living with just one specialised business. This is can be seen in the 1845 Kelly's directory, where it lists Sarah Smith as both the innkeeper of the Bridge Inn, which also acted as a coal exchange. Then there was also Charles William Towner, brewer of the White Hart Inn, who was also a coal merchant and a butcher. Even the larger partnership of Cole and Catt were trading as both coal and wine and spirit merchants. This raises an interesting question; what is the connection if any between coal and beer? Perhaps we will never know but it is intriguing. Perhaps these were the only meeting places where you could obtain change without banks. (It was not until 1855, that there is a bank in Newhaven included in a directory; the London and Counties.) Another change in the 1845 directory is that Mr John Hubard is no longer a school master, but still has a number of trades; he was now a grocer, draper, bookseller and a stationer. These examples just show how hard life was in pre railway Newhaven.5

From about 1870, this part of Newhaven High Street shows Reeves Stationer & post master (successor to Mr Camp) - now branch of HSBC Bank; S Noakes, grocer - now Boots Chemists; and S Corbett, general store - now Newhaven Photographic & Chemist.

Picture courtesy of Newhaven Museum

Higher up the social order in 1831, there were three surgeons listed, which classified them as gentry, possibly because they had a profession and were not trade. One of these surgeons, Mr John Noakes, showed in a later directory that he supplemented his income by combining his medical career with that of being an insurance agent![6] Within a decade, two of the surgeons had left the town and do not appear again in any later directory or census.

Other changes that took place was that one of the grocers and drapers, Mr John Camp, had become insolvent and filed for bankruptcy, which is surprising as he had also been the Towns Post Master.[7] However, it may be that over the years he had gradually gone deaf, and so was unable to continue his business. There is a note of a John Camp in the Workhouse about this time. If you could not support yourself during this time, the only option was the workhouse and all the indignities that it brought with it. However for Mr Camp it was not quite this straightforward, his fall from businessman to pauper had a twist. Today we would consider that he had a nervous breakdown, yet to the Victorians at this time he was considered an eccentric. According to reports, although he and his wife ran the shop, Mr Camp would sometimes go off for months rambling with the gypsies. Then, for about two years, he became very lazy and never left his bed. We do not know what happened to his wife but in the end Mr Camp was living in a cave, never shaving and surviving on charity. In the end he was found starving and dying. He was taken to the workhouse but died shortly afterwards.[8]

The next post master in 1855 was George Smith, another man who was very much multi-tasking, being a bank manager, an insurance agent and also the registrar of births, deaths and marriages. He was followed as post master by Jack Reeves, the chemist, druggist and stationer.

This shows that, at the end of the Georgian period and beginning of the Victorian, life in Newhaven was hard, even for those with their own businesses. It should also be pointed out that the town was cut off from the rest of the county, as were many towns and villages in Sussex. This was mainly due to most roads running from north to south, with very few covering the east to west routes. Road communication was poor and, although a new toll road had been built in 1825 from Brighton, it ended at Newhaven. If you wanted to make an onward journey to Eastbourne there was no maintained road. During the winter it is possible that the roadway would have been muddy and highly rutted or even hidden under snow and, at best, the journey would have been very slow and uncomfortable. The best way to travel inland would have been by barge along the River

Ouse or by sea to other coastal towns. Even the delivery of mail was only once a day until 1866, when it increased to three times a day, like other larger towns of Sussex.

The aforementioned early directories also included some traders that we would not have expected in late Georgian or early Victorian period. Some businesses that would have been traditionally run by men, were owned by women. This could have been because their husbands had died, in which case they would sometimes take over and successfully run the business for many years. Newhaven had four such women in the 1830's; a blacksmiths and farriers was run by Mrs William (Lydia) Adam, Ann Stone, who was both a plumber and glazier, Sarah Tubb the grocer and, of course, the aforementioned Sarah who ran the Bridge Inn very successfully for many years.

It is clear from the 1841 census for Newhaven that the majority of the people listed were born in Sussex, with only around 12% of the population coming from outside the county. [9] Of the 950 individuals in Newhaven at this time, 115 were born outside Sussex, including forty one women and children and around thirty five men of a working age from outside the area. The rest of the non-Sussex born men were termed as "of independent means".

This census has some basic detail and shows how those from outside the area were an integral part of the local community, although some did work that was not carried out by Sussex men. All twelve men who were working for H M Coast Guard came from outside Sussex, as did the minister of the dissenting church. There was also the only cooper, victualler, school master, wheelwright, navvy and a surgeon's apprentice, all with a tick indicating they were not born in the county. Two of those listed were indeed actual foreigners; the surgeons apprentice and the navvy. However, there is no information about their actual place of birth. All the others were working in the same trades as the locally born inhabitants. Some of those listed, may have married a local woman, like the wheelwright Mr Duly, and therefore set up business in the wife's home town rather than their own place of birth.

Of the local population as many as seventy were classed as labourers and a further twenty five were agricultural labourers. Being a sea port, there were fifteen mariners, of whom half a dozen were not locally born (the rest may have been at sea on census day), with a further nine men working in various ship building trades, although the only actual ship builder, John Gray, came from outside Sussex. In addition to these, the river and sea meant employment for seven pilots, three watermen and a barge master. From these examples it can be seen that both the land and sea gave employment to a large majority of the working population.

Although, at the time men, would have been the main bread winners, there were still a few women in employment. These included forty female servants whose ages ranged from fourteen to Elizabeth Vigar aged sixty five. There were also trades that women only would have pursued, such as the four dressmakers and two laundresses. There were, however, two listed as business owners as mentioned earlier; grocer, Sarah Tubb and Sarah Smith the innkeeper.[10] Sarah Smith lived until she was 74, having been the 'respected landlady' of the Bridge Inn for 50 years, dying in 1864.[11]

A drawing possibly dating from 1798 shows"Hero" the thrice weekly stage coach that ran between Brighton and Hastings, stopping at the Bridge Hotel in Newhaven.

From the slide collection of the late Tony Payne

This, though, was an age when it was the men who worked. Yet, of these, there were only twelve male servants. The rest of the male population was engaged in some kind of retail trade, manufacture, agriculture or maritime trade. These jobs and trades ranged from a beer seller and three innkeepers, to a saddler and his apprentice son as well as six shoe makers assisted by four journeymen shoemakers.

There was the odd anomaly found when cross checking the historical records. Some of the trades listed in this census, did not agree with the local trade directory of 1839.[12] Examples of this discrepancy are the saddle maker and Mr Kemp the watch maker. Of course, this could be either because on the printing date of the directory, that they were only visiting or were away on the day of the census.

Although virtually all those listed in the census were earning some kind of living, there were still some forty eight people in the workhouse. Unfortunately, the 1841 records do not state who in the workhouse was from Newhaven, so we are unable to see if there was full employment. This information would not to be expected from the census compilers.[13] Fortunately, there are records available in the County Record Office which, by comparing with the census, make it possible to look further into this matter. At the time of the census, there were just 5 people from Newhaven in the workhouse, and all were women. Of these, we would class two of them as children who had been left there by their mother. Also, with no old people's homes or other hospital available, two of the women had nowhere else to go. Only one of the women would have been capable of work, as she had been a servant but at that time had no work. Perhaps the most interesting inmate was Sarah Deane, who has a note in her admission record that her father had been transported. She was aged just 13 and came from East Blatchington (Seaford).[14]

Some other research has been carried out on the next census of 1851. From that, it appears that, of the adults (those over 12 years old), there were just three women and one man from Newhaven in the Workhouse. It is possible that the women there were servants who had children, as there were children under 5 there as well.[15] At this time, if a servant had a child outside marriage, she would lose her job and have no means of supporting herself except the workhouse.

The Downs Hospital in 1990 prior to the partial demolition and re-development. It was the Newhaven Union Workhouse built in 1835

Courtesy of Newhaven Museum

Chapter 2.
A developing Town.

There were some interesting, if not very complimentary, comments made about Newhaven as it grew from a town of about 900 people in 1841 to a large port and railway town housing over 6500 by 1891. In fact, there was only one complimentary view recorded, which was in 1889, stating that, although growing the developments were pleasing to look at, 'Newhaven... A street over which Ruskin may have rejoiced, so irregular are the houses, and gables, and quaint chimney stacks.'[16]

The Victorian period saw a rise in the middle and upper classes, together with their aspirations for themselves and their families. They were starting to look to move out of the smoky cities in which they had made their fortunes and risen in prestige. More of the rising middle classes were moving to watering places, where they could parade in parks or in other open spaces away from the lower orders so that they would be noticed. With their new money, they were able to emanate the upper classes looking for a more comfortable lifestyle.

Unfortunately, although Newhaven became a major port and starting point for trips to the continent, it never became one of those places the more affluent would want to have been seen in. That is not to say there were not affluent people living in Newhaven, it was just not a town to move to. As the town grew, no squares were built or green spaces designed, which is what ladies and gentlemen desired to walk in and look elegant.

Newhaven seems to have grown in rather a piecemeal way, with developers adding housing without worrying about any grand plan. This lack of planned development is not surprising, as a report published in an 1889 newspaper shows that it was not part of the London, Brighton and South Coast railway's policy to develop it as a watering place. However, they had no objections to Mr Cyrus Legge, a shareholder, starting a company to develop the town and even offered assistance to him. However, nothing appears to have come of this and his name does not appear again.[17] It was not even the old land owners who set about building and expanding the town, but those who came later to try and make a profit by adding value to their newly acquired landholding.

Newhaven was a town that grew as and when individual developers felt that they could make a profit by building a street or two. Some of the published views of the town were very negative because of this random expansion of the town, such as in 1904:- 'Of Newhaven there is little to say, except that in rough weather the traveller from France is very glad to reach it, and on a fine day the traveller from England is happy to leave it behind.'[18] Another, equally disparaging, remark came from the pen of Charles Dickens in 1876, the son of the famous author; 'It has that forlorn here-to-day-and-gone-to-morrow look peculiar to places afflicted with a customs-house.'[19]

Not only was it not going to be thought of as a watering place; 'Nothing prevents Newhaven from becoming a first-rate watering place, but its water',[20] it seems that even more important buildings, such as the London and Paris Hotel built by the London, Brighton and South Coast Railway, did nothing to improve this poor impression. This hotel was a major building that was, unfortunately, constructed with a lack of thought to some important design details. Although they offered moderate tariffs in order to persuade travellers to stay, travel guides of the day thought that it was better to avoid the place; 'as though people went regularly to Newhaven as to other watering-places; but this seems incredible.'[21] Part of the complaint about the hotel, was that it was built virtually on the wooden pier. In other words, working men would be seen from the dining room window, which was not something the patrons, especially the ladies, would wish to see.

A view of the London and Paris Hotel from the late 1870's or 1880's showing PS Bordeaux moored at the hotel's pier.

Courtesy of Newhaven Museum

These quotes from journals and newspaper articles are very much in contrast with the impression put out by those who were selling property in the town. From these, we read of an exciting up and coming town that is growing and becoming the place not only to live in, but also to invest in. For example, in 1840, some years before the railway was due to come there was a substantial house in St Luke's Lane with an 100 foot garden, 2 parlours and the "appropriate sleeping accommodation", which was now for sale by auction and a "must buy". It was stated that the "property has of late been greatly enhanced in value at Newhaven-decidedly the most improving Sea Port in Sussex".22

St Luke's Lane about 1956 from the High Street with St Luke's Cottages on the left.

Courtesy of Newhaven Museum

Similarly, other sales of houses in the town show that many were large with numerous rooms. Back in 1820 a substantial property was sold in Newhaven High Street that is hard to believe ever existed, knowing the street today. For a small rent this building was advertised as either suitable for trade of a family residence. This is not surprising as it consisted of two parlours in the front, a kitchen, a cellar, five bedrooms, a warehouse, stables, a garden and a private entrance to the High Street. It is a pity that there was no indication as to its exact location, but it does indicate that Newhaven's Town centre had some large properties, both shops and houses, in the period prior the Queen Victoria's accession.23

All the later sales notices were in a similar vain. For example, in 1865 when William Elphick was selling some of his building land along the river bank, buyers were told this was 'a rare opportunity for the erection of quays, wharves, etc. together with several eligible sites for the erection of Villa Residences, with an excellent approach from the Lewes Road by carriage drive; beautifully situate, with a southern aspect'.[24]

Not only is it not possible to find out whom the builder was of the two, relatively new freehold houses in St John's Place, but also the location is not shown on any known map. All that is available to us is the 1866 sale advertisement, which was very positive about them. They were being sold with respectable tenants and, as the advert stated, Newhaven was the place to be. "It is a patent fact, that when government patronizes a town or tradesmen, the fortune of that town and that of the tradesmen may be considered made...Land is in great request, The Railway and the Packet Service combined, constitute it one of the most rising towns in Sussex."[25] This immediate growth in population can also be seen by the fact that a new chapel had just been built in the centre of Newhaven.

At this point in time, a new bridge had just been built over the river, coinciding with the completion of the work for a new cut which divided the river, improving navigation. In 1863 The Government passed legislation permitting funding for work on straightening the river. This would allow better inland access to Lewes and well as helping alleviate the need to keep dredging the river so that larger ships could dock. By straightening of the river Ouse we have Denton Island to the side of the main river. This piece of Victorian engineering took four years to complete and is said to have cost £30,000 at the time a huge sum of money.[26]

Even after the railway came and the harbour improved to take larger ships including the cross channel ferry service was completed, the town was slow to develop. This may have been because the main land owners took time to agree to changes in the ownership of land which would then free it up for development. It was only after the Acts of Enclosure were agreed that it was possible to allow the freeholds of any new houses built to be sold.[27] This modern form of house sale could not happen in the parish of Newhaven before 1848. Without clear ownership of land brought about by the Acts of Enclosure, sales were complicated by appearances in manorial courts, where each change was registered. Enclosure did away with this meaning that just a simple conveyance was required, which also speeded up sales by clarifying exactly who owned what piece of land.

By 1841, the largest land owner in Newhaven were the William Elphick's, these were father and son usually known as the elder and younger. According to the tithe map produced in 1841 the Lord of the Manor of Newhaven was the Earl of Sheffield who owned 374 acres of land, while William Elphick, owned 459 acres between them in Newhaven.[28] In Denton, the next parish across the River Ouse at this time it was the Earl of Chichester who was the Lord of the Manor who had the large land holding, the only other land owner of note was William Henry Bates most of whose land bordered on to the town of Newhaven.[29]

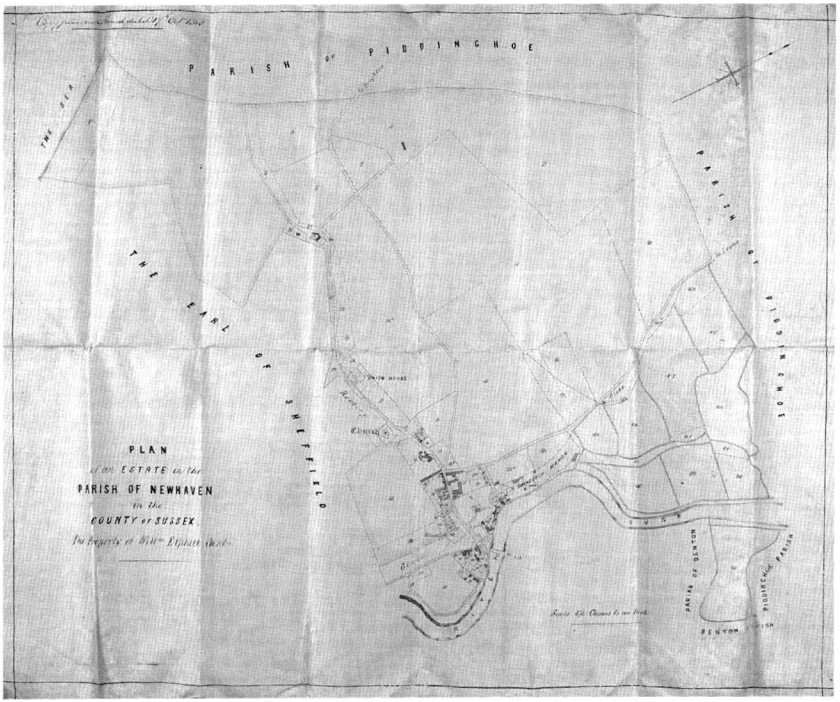

A plan of Newhaven dated 17 October 1848 showing the land holding of William Elphick following the Act of Enclosure, which confirmed that he was the largest land holder in the Parish. Courtesy of The Keep (formerly ESRO. P426/2

From documents held in the East Sussex Record Office, it is clear that the Earl of Sheffield was not able to sell his Newhaven estate until the passing of the Settled Lands Acts of 1882 and 1890.[30] This was not a restriction that would affect other land owners such as William Elphick. However, other records show that although William

Elphick the Younger was selling land from this time, he was not going to risk his capital by investing in house building. By 1852 he had moved to the recently developed Kemp Town area of Brighton which had become a desirable area where a man calling himself a gentleman would want to live.31 He was, however, still living on the rents of his Newhaven and Piddinghoe lands that he was still letting out as farmland. Part of the reason that Kemp Town was desirable and Newhaven was not, was because there were squares for the ladies and gentlemen to parade and relax in Brighton.

Though land was required for housing in 1847, when the railway finally arrived in the town, there did not seem to be anyone willing to invest in housing development. In 1848, William Elphick tried to sell an area which was then known as The Knowles but it was not until 1854 that he finally sold any of it that would be used for building. John Bennett Lee was the initial developer of part of this estate, building over 40 houses in South Eastern Terrace Chapel Road, South Eastern Cottages Chapel Road, Sussex Place Chapel Road and Sussex Square as well as The Chapel in Chapel Road.32 The chapel referred to was the Wesleyan Methodist Chapel. Much of this development is under the modern centre of Newhaven and the ring road South Way.

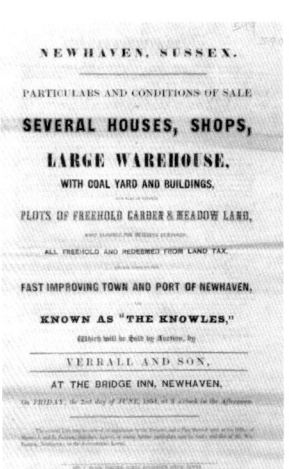

(Left) The particulars of sale of William Elphick's "The Knowles" part of his Newhaven estate, auctioned at the Bridge Inn 2nd June 1854.

Courtesy of The Keep ACC3412/3/590

(Right) This is the sale particulars of Meeching Place Estate, auctioned on 22 November 1870 at the White Hart Inn Lewes.

Courtesy of The Keep ACC3412/5/4/3A

There is a small but interesting note included with the documents stored in the East Sussex Record Office relating to the ownership of the land after it was sold by Mr Elphick. It states that, on the death of Mr Stevens, who must have been the first purchaser of this part of the estate, it was transferred 'to Zacharias Stevens, his nephew, and John Bennett Lee of Newhaven, builder, his cousin', thus forming a link to how Mr Lee became involved in local development. Although Mr Lee was a carpenter by trade, he later classed himself as a builder, having developed a number of streets and houses.[33]

Following the second major auction in 1854 there was still quite a lot of land that remained unsold, which was still of value to the original owner, as he could use it as collateral for loans. This appears to be what William Elphick was doing. It was not until the late 1870's that, not only more was land sold, but a major new road had been laid out; Meeching Road. It was referred to as a new road in 1878 when a property there was sold by Mr Lower to Mr William Bodle. From this sale it is clear that the road did not exist when Simpson Lower bought some land in the Knowles in 1874 from Mr William Henry Standing, who, a few years earlier, purchased it from Mr Elphick. Therefore it is clear that it was Simpson Lower who was also a major developer of Newhaven in the Meeching Road area from about 1874.[34]

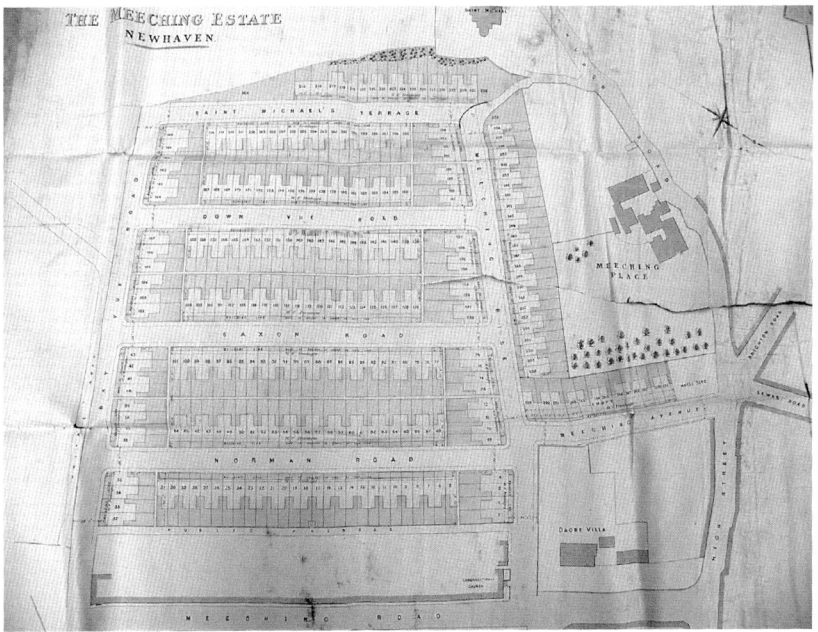

Plan of the Meeching Estate, Newhaven drawn up by Samuel Denman surveyor in September 1896.　　　　　　　　　　　Courtesy of The Keep - HIL/9/14

On the other side of the river, sales of land for housing were also taking place, but again sellers had to wait for the demand for housing to rise enough to make it profitable. There may have been a demand for accommodation but the navvies and labourers who came to build the railway and improve the harbour could only rent low cost housing. This would have been why many of them appeared to be living in huts. With no demand for accommodation at rental prices that would give an income to the builders and developers, few houses were built at this time. Returns on income for those with money to invest would be far less from land than by prudent investment in government and other stock at this time. Therefore, there was a delay in house building for many years.[35]

James Lower had bought a number of acres of land in Denton, possibly in the 1860s, which he used as collateral for mortgages until 1880, when he sold the land on to London couple, Mr & Mrs Bond. Unusually for this period, there was a further trust deed referred to in the surviving paperwork, which stated that Mr Bond transferred this land to his wife 'for her separate use independent of her husband'.[36] This may have been unusual but Mrs Bond was a true entrepreneur and she knew an opportunity when she saw it.

It was shortly after the purchase was completed that Mrs Bond started to borrowed large sums of money to develop her housing estate. She borrowed about two thousand pounds from various people to build Clifton Terrace and East View Cottages, about twenty houses which she either sold or let out. According to one set of deeds, she borrowed £800 as a mortgage from Hugh Gorringe, Peter Rollins Gorringe and Richard Ryder, to pay for the construction of two houses in Clifton Terrace plus a further four in East View Cottages. It would be interesting to know how she got a return on this investment in these houses.

Others building houses were the Catt family, who built houses in Denton Terrace and well as an area known as High Street Miss Catt Cottages. Caroline Catt was a member of the Catt family of Bishopstone and, over time, they built up a large landholding in Newhaven and Denton. By the late nineteenth century she was selling land to both the railway and the harbour companies. In fact, by 1882, Caroline Catt had become a much more important figure

Taken in Jan 2014 this is the front of the old workhouse later the it was the Downs Hospital. It is about to become housing.

Taken in in late 2012 when the walls separating the men's from the women's sections of the workhouse had been removed prior to re-development.

St Luke's Lane from the High Street the lane leads to the car park in Lower Place. In 2012 when the picture was taken the library is on the left and former Woolworth's store on the right was a discount shop.

A view of Chapel Street taken in 2012. Somewhere near here would have been Church Road

Meeching Road taken in 2013 from Hill Side.

Clifton Road taken in 2012, this was part of the area developed by Mrs Bond her Clifton Terrace has since disappeared.

The junction of Lewes Road and Brighton Road as it is in 2012.

Taken in June 2012 on a flight over Newhaven showing how built up the town is today, but how little shipping use the harbour.

Looking toward the original ship yards from Denton Island in 2013. Part of the old shipyard site in Robinson Road is now a depot for refuse collection vehicles. There is still though an active slipway for the current yards.

The High Street taken in 1964 when cars could drive there.

Courtesy of the late Tony Payne's slide collection.

The top of the High Street from Brighton Road a cinema used to be near the sign for the car park. Taken in the 1960's.

Courtesy of the late Tony Payne's slide collection.

Another 1960's view of Newhaven High Street - not a charity shop in site!

Courtesy of the late Tony Payne's slide collection.

locally, as by then she, 'is or claims to be entitled as lady of the Manor of Denton Sussex.'37

On the Newhaven side, part of a field once known as Holmes Field was sold in 1866 to Simpson Lower, who was recorded as a being a baker of Newhaven. It appears that, having bought the land, he then sold it on to others who would develop it. As part of the conditions attached to the sale he stipulated that the owner must maintain the drains and that any building must be at least twenty five feet from the road. The original site of what was Holmes Field is now under Elphick Road, Brighton Road and Lewes Road.

It was still not easy to sell land for house building. From the proposed sale advertised in 1866, of the 95 plots of land making up the Brighton and Lewes Roads area, it seems that only 42 were actually sold at that time.38 It would be interesting to find out when he was able to sell the rest of this land.

In 1976 work started on the Brighton Road / Lewes Road junction to make the ring road around the town.

Courtesy of Newhaven Museum

Chapter 3.
All Change by 1881.

Between the 1841 and 1881 censuses, a major change in employment along with a growth in population had taken place.[39] This was due to the railway coming from Brighton via Lewes in 1847, and, a few years later in 1864, it was extended a couple of extra miles to Seaford. Throughout this whole period, the harbour was being improved, not only for the regular packet boat service to France (at one time there was four paddle-steamers and two steamships operating on the route) but also a twice weekly service to Jersey in 1850. Following a number of government reports, improvements had been made which also meant that the port had been upgraded to become an official port of refuge in times of storms. Over the years more and more ships unloaded their cargos at the warehouses that had recently appeared along the river bank at Newhaven. Although the cross channel service began in 1849, due to legal constraints it was suspended until the Paris Exhibition in 1851, when the ferry service it really took off.[40]

This is an 1878 drawing of the proposed harbour improvements, by Fred D Banister. Taken from "A Modern History of Newhaven Harbour, with proposals for its improvement." Published in London by Letts & Son & Co in 1879

With the transfer of what was known as the cross channel packet boat service from Shoreham to Newhaven, alongside the railway, industrialisation came to a rural and maritime community. This change in importance of the town to an international port meant that, even though there were still men working on the land, the overall the numbers were less than before. Twenty five men were listed as agricultural labourers, with a further four as shepherds. There was a farm bailiff also listed; George Kemp. This job had not been separately included forty years earlier, when the same number of men appeared to be working on farms. However, by 1881, half of them had been elsewhere, reflecting the growing population brought about by the availability of work in Newhaven.

As previously mentioned, according to the 1841 census, very few women were classified as working and most of those were servants. By 1881 this had changed, not dramatically but there was a noticeable number who were now working. Amongst those who took up employment, at least one was employed in a new trade that had not existed forty years earlier; a telegraphist, Elizabeth King. Few jobs at that time would have been unisex, which means finding them is not easy. Occasionally it is possible to find trades which employed both men and women and, even though it was possible for the sexes to work together, it was still rare. Two women and two men were recorded as being employed as accounts clerks. There was also an assistant postmistress. Although there was a female assistant overseer, her duties would have been to deal with the women inmates of the workhouse, while the overseer had charge of the whole establishment. There was also the traditional job of teaching which included women as well as school masters but the men probably taught at a higher level.

The change in place of birth goes much further than just those who worked on the land. There was a general shortage of labour in the town that was caused by more shipping coming into the port and the extension of the railway. Part of the reason for this would have been that the increased work load required many new skills that those who had worked on land would not have had. It was those who had learned how to service the new age of steam that were required in the new engineering establishments that evolved to service the ships and trains that now came to Newhaven.

An example of this was in 1851, when an advertisement was placed for shipbuilders in newspapers across the region. This was because Mr Gray required a further 20 skilled hands for the enlarged and enhanced shipyard he owned.[41] For a short period after his death in 1855, ship building seemed to come to an end. This may be because it took time to sell the yard and for the new owners to obtain contracts to build new ships. By the time the 1858 directory was published, the ship and boat yards were in full production, possibly having grown three fold, including John Wingfield as a boat builder, William Stevens a shipwright and W H Courtney as the ship builder. In fact, it was reported that, by 1859, Newhaven was building 500 ton gunboats for the Royal Navy. Again, there was a break in ship building sometime around 1864 when the yard was sold again.42

John Gray's ship yard was situated in the Robinson Road area of Newhaven, from where some time around 1860 this photo was take.

Courtesy of Newhaven Museum

By the time of the 1881 census the railway in Newhaven had been well established for some years, the harbour expanded and the continental ferry service was popular with travellers. The town had bonded and other new warehouses which had been built to cope with the increase in general sea trade. This meant that many new trades and skills were required to keep these enterprises going. Although the railway was only an extension of the main line from London to Brighton, men were still required to run many aspects of the railway locally, together with the ferry services both to France two or three times a day and to Jersey a couple times a week. The Dieppe and Jersey packet boats, like much of the shipping that now used the harbour, were steam powered, meaning new skills were also required to run them.

It was the new skills that came with industrialisation that show a big change in the nature of employment. All the boiler makers, together with their apprentices, had recently come to Newhaven. Likewise, the eleven engine drivers living in the town and the thirteen engine fitters all were born elsewhere. The same was true for virtually all the engineering trades, either on land or associated with shipping. An exception to this were two of the ships carpenters, who were born in the town. There was also a gasworks and although only the foreman is recorded as being employed there, some of the engineers may have worked there as well. For some reason, only one gasfitter was listed.

Traditional skills were still required even with modern industry. As a huge number of workers was required, both skilled and unskilled men carried out these tasks. There were some one hundred men working in the building industry, which included carpenters, decorators and bricklayers, with a further 274 classed as general labourers. The sea had always been a big employer of labour and mariners accounted for about one hundred and twenty five men.

A period drawing of Newhaven looking east over the River Ouse showing the railway and harbour in it's hay day.

Courtesy of Newhaven Museum

NEWHAVEN, FROM THE EAST.

The railway did employ labourers and porters who had been born in the town but there were very few of them. Likewise, the dock employed a few local men as stevedores. Overall this shows that the original local population from a few decades earlier had accepted and worked alongside the new residents who had only recently made Newhaven their home. It is clear from the census that many of the locals had married outsiders, which is why so many of the traditional family names carried on.

Alongside the expected range of employment opportunities that were listed in 1881, there is a surprise. To that date, there was no reference to a theatre in Newhaven, although there is evidence of an early cinema. However, this census shows that there were three actors either living or staying in the town at that time. From the newspapers, it appears that, from the 1860's until the late 1880's, there was, indeed, a theatre.[43] In 1865 it was the Alexandra Theatre run by a Mr T R Scott, while in 1886 the Victoria Theatre was advertising the variety artists in Mr Paul Courtney's troupe.

Young people also had more choice of work by the eighteen eighties. Schooling had yet to become compulsorily past the age of 10 or 11, although there was provision for it until the age of 13. Of the 14 year olds listed there were four errand boys, one errand girl, and two office boys. Other trades also included boys who were not classified as apprentices, such as a steam tug boy. The plasterer's boy, Walter Redman, was youngest recorded at 13. Children were starting to have a longer childhood, as well as, at least, the basics of education. However, this may not have been universally accepted as on the French ships in harbour on the day of the census, it was recorded that boys as young as 11 were working on them.

A Victorian period drawing of the High Street. The Blue Anchor would be behind us, with the White Hart in front to the right with writing on its side wall. Further along on the left is The Ship Inn and the Bridge Hotel at the bottom of the street.

Courtesy of Newhaven Museum

Parts of society had, by this time, become wealthier and this was reflected in some of the businesses that existed to serve the new customers and trades that could be termed luxury rather than necessary were now in Newhaven. For example, the town could boast four gardeners, one of whom classed himself as a master gardener, and a sweet shop keeper. Whereas other hotels may not have required the luxury of a receptionist, the London and Paris Hotel employed a female one, as well as waiters. On the domestic front, there were two governesses employed as well as half a dozen nurse maids. Such an influx of residents meant that there were now also two policemen employed.

Beer houses and inns flourished in Newhaven in the 1880's, supported by the three brewers. Found, so far, as licensed to sell alcohol, are four beer retailers and two beer house keepers, one of whom doubled up as a labourer. The number of inns and hotels had also increased. Joining the Bridge Inn which had always been a hotel (and at various times had been called the Bridge Hotel, was the aforementioned, recently opened London and Paris Hotel. The other inns listed included, The Ship Hotel, The White Hart Inn, The Hope Inn and The Ark Inn.

According to the census, there were a number of beer retailers but the names of the premises they ran was not listed. Amongst these retailers were two who were both carpenters and beer-sellers, Charles Trow in Elphick Road and James Woolgar in Chapel Street. There was also a barge owner and beer retailer called Charles Stone in Essex Square. Therefore we can be sure that there were other outlets which sold beer and other beverages besides the ones names in that census.

Bridge Street looking towards Woolgars Passage (on left) with the High Street at the end. Bridge Street was full of individual shops, all with plenty of trade.

Courtesy of Newhaven Museum

The number of shops had increased and, going by the numbers of staff employed in them, the premises were larger as well. There were eleven bakers who, between them, were employing six assistants and a baker's boy. In Chapel Street, one greengrocer was also trading as an eating house keeper, while there were also four additional grocers together with the four that were listed as both grocers and drapers. At this time, Mr Stone was recorded as just a draper although, according to later records, he is also a grocer. One of the largest increases in retailing were the butchers' shops, with nine now in Newhaven. Most of these traders were employing assistants as well, so there was plenty of opportunity to find work.

Some of the business in the town had become quite large, with five employers living in the town who were employing nine or more men and boys. The largest was William Hobbs who was the tenant farmer of Court House Farm and was employed 35 men plus 18 boys. Of the other large employers, three were in the building trade. Albert King was employing twenty five men, builders merchant, Edmond Baker, employed eighteen and Mark Woolgar, another builder, engaged eleven men.

Amongst the growing businesses was James Bannister's the grocery retailer, who had built up his business to the extent that he had eight men and a boy working for him in 1881. Not only had he expanded his grocery business to employ more staff, his premises was now a purpose built shop and warehouse which had been built in 1880.[44] Later, even more of the high street was taken over by the firm and it was said that Newhaven had "bannisters on both sides of the High Street".

The ownership of various shops and businesses within the town, also show how the town had changed. These include George Brooker who, in the previous 1841, census was a tailor's apprentice, but was now a tailor employing four men. From another local family there was Emma Towner, classed as a butcher's wife running a large butchers shop with two men and boy in her employ.[45] Sadly, she had taken over the butchers shop as her husband was now in an asylum and died there a couple of years later. Also, Charles Woolgar from another old Newhaven family, was now a blacksmith with three men as employees.

Some retail trades had not been required until the town grew so large, including an egg salesman, three milkmen, a fish salesman and a postman. If residents wanted something a bit more luxurious, there was also an oyster merchant. For some years, Newhaven had had an oyster trade, most of which was exported to France. However, in 1877 a new company came to the town to take over the trade, under the management of Tom Holden, and the Anglo-Portuguese Oyster Company began trading. They leased additional land at

Sleepers Hole adjoining the harbour.[46] On the more professional side there were two solicitors and two surgeons and a professor of music, who lived at 34 Meeching Road, sharing the house with a school master and his family.[47]

Looking across Sleepers Hole towards the London and Paris Hotel.

from the authors own collection

Some of the women who had to work were also becoming more specialised in the skills they could offer, though there were still numerous dressmakers and laundresses. Now, however there was also a shirt maker, a milliner, two needlewomen and two mangle women, not forgetting the half dozen or so women who were shopkeepers in their own right. Enjoying, perhaps, more glamorous employment were two stewardess's on the steamships who may have worked alongside three male stewards.

Not only did the ranges of jobs change but also where the residents came from, which is not that surprising, bearing in mind the growth in population. It is possible that the twice weekly boat service to Jersey had brought about an influx of people from that island as forty of those now living in the town were born in Jersey. Others came to the town from all over the country, including as far away as Scotland and Cornwall, to find work in a growing town.

Many of these were practicing trades that would have been new to the town, but where now required due to the changes there. With so much trade going on, there were now half a dozen carters and carriers, only two of whom were boarders and may not have lived in Newhaven. For relaxation for the more middle class residents, there was a coffee house, which the census shows employed a coffee house keeper and a manager. This shows that Newhaven was now a much more diverse and busy urban centre than it had been previously.

Meeching Road, a late Victorian drawing showing it as a street the middle classes would prefer to live.

Courtesy of Newhaven Museum

Part 2 Stories from the newspapers.

**Chapter 4
A New Queen.**

Like everywhere else, the inhabitants of Newhaven were ready to celebrate events of national local importance, especially if drink was included. They were a relatively loyal town's folk and had a connection with Royalty from the days of Regency Britain. This connection related to when George IV, who enjoyed a good drink while staying at the Brighton. Orders were placed two or three times a week supplies of Tipper Ale to be delivered to his Majesty. Thomas Tipper's Ales were very famous in their day and continued to be so even after Mr Tipper's death, when Mr Brooker and Mr T Stone, followed by G Stone and R Towner, continued to brew them.[48] In fact, there are references to this beer in the books, Bleak House and Nicholas Nickleby by Charles Dickens.

It was on 28th June 1838 that a young Queen Victoria had her coronation in Westminster Abbey. She was crowned a year after succeeding to the thrown following the death on the 20th June 1837 of her uncle William IV. This new beginning was celebrated by large crowds in London and other cities and towns throughout the Kingdom.

The celebration in Newhaven following the coronation was aimed at bringing the inhabitants of this small town together. It was a time of rejoicing and must have taken a great deal of planning to ensure that it was as good as, if not better, than the events held in nearby towns. An interesting aspect of it was that the gentry served the lower classes during the main part of the public event, which comprised of a communal dinner followed by suitable entertainment.

The dinner itself took place on the cricket ground near the town for those that were, termed in the reports as "the poor". The cricket ground mentioned is not the one we know of today, nor is it one of today's recreation grounds. That is because the Cricket ground was donated by the Earl of Sheffield, with the first recorded match taking place in 1890. By the word poor, the good ladies and gentlemen of the town would have meant all those who were in work as an employee or servant, not those in the workhouse.

Enough tables were laid out to cater for 600 men, women and children. It was stated in the newspapers that good English fare was served, which was served by the ladies and carved by the gentlemen of the town. Besides this, ample ale was supplied from the three booths set up, one for each of the local inns. By today's standards, a lot of free ale was provided, but again it should be remembered that, at that time, it was safer to drink beer than water. Each man was given a quart while the women had half a quart each. Children were not left out as the under 16's also received a quarter of pint of beer each. It may possible be, that they were given double this amount, depending on which newspaper report is to be believed.

To give a festive feel to the day, all the tables were decorated with flags and flowers. When the meal came to an end, 400 gooseberry pies were distributed to the children plus some other foodstuffs. These were supplied by Mr William Cole, who traded as a grocer, and a local Lloyd's agent. Following the food, there was dancing and sports held on the green with music provided by the Seaford band.

The Newhaven Workhouse in a prominent site near the Church as a warning to the lower orders of what can happen to them if they do not behave in the manor expected of them.

Courtesy of Newhaven Museum

CHURCH, RECTORY, AND UNION, NEWHAVEN.

After the lower orders had been fed and the entertainment for the town's folk came to an end, it was time for the upper classes and gentry to retire and enjoy themselves. They dined with entertainment in the evening at the Bridge Inn, where a room was provided for the continuation of entertainment in the form of a singing. It was reported that, once the tables were cleared, a number of toasts were drunk, including the royal toast.

Those in the workhouse were not left out of the celebration. They were given roast beef, plum pudding, and strong beer by the guardians of the workhouse.[49] These would have been rare treats for those who were unfortunate enough to find themselves in this institution. This would have been nothing like the usual food at a workhouse, where strict limits were usually placed on the amount an inmate was allowed to eat. In fact, a letter was written in February 1836 asking for permission to increase the daily food rations in the workhouse from 12 to 16 ounces of bread for men and 10 to 14 ounces for women, with no change for children. In addition, this request also included increasing the amount of tea and sugar for those able bodied women who worked within the workhouse to the same amount old people over 60 received. So, the coronation meal was a real treat for them.[50]

In contrast to this great celebration for the young Queen's coronation, the following year there was a much smaller party for her marriage. In February 1840 Queen Victoria married Prince Albert and, although places like Brighton held large parties, Newhaven was relatively quiet. It may well have been that too much had been lavished on the previous year's celebration.

The ships in the harbour were duly decorated with colourful flags. Then at, 12 noon, Mr T Stone, the Queen's brewer of "Tipper Ale", did what was expected of him. A large vat of beer that had been renamed for the day as "Victoria" was put out; "the Queen's brewer, gave several buckets of good old tipper beer to any person who chose to drink the Queen's health". It can be assumed that this was a popular gesture. Later, as the evening approached, only three businesses illuminated their premises as a sign of loyalty; W.M. Stone and Son, Mr George Stone and Mrs Smith of the Bridge Inn. Later the Bridge Inn was the setting for a ball that carried on until late at night, at the end of which the Queen and Prince Albert's health was toasted.[51] On this occasion, it was noted in the Sussex Advertiser that the "rejoicing was on a limited scale"[52]

The following year the Bridge Inn was, again, the focus of the celebration in the town on the occasion of the birth of the Prince of Wales. The boys of the town were given tar barrels to burn to show the towns loyalty alongside a firework display and the ever popular proprietress of The Bridge Inn, Mrs Smith, provided the "flowing bowl" for the tradesmen of the town to celebrate.53

Edward VII's coronation celebrations in August 1902. This took place in the High Street with Bannister's shop to the right.

Courtesy Newhaven Museum

≈≈≈≈≈≈≈≈≈

Those who were unfortunate enough to end up in Newhaven Workhouse may not have fared as badly as those in workhouses elsewhere. There is proof that, occasionally, treats were given to the inmates there. One fine day in early May 1864, a meal of roast beef and plum pudding was provided by an anonymous donor. Besides the good food, tobacco was distributed to the men at the discretion of the guardians, while the women and children were given oranges, nuts and sweetmeats. The children were also given toys.54

≈≈≈≈≈≈≈≈≈

The ladies and gentlemen of the town liked to celebrate and they made sure that the newspapers of the day heard about their dinners. One was held in 1839, when the firm of Cole Catt & Co launched their new ship, the Louisa, when it was reported that the loyal toasts included those to the Queen and her mother.

≈≈≈≈≈≈≈≈≈

Finally on the subject of loyal celebration came the marriage of the Prince of Wales in 1864, who was later to become King Edward VII. On the 10th March 1863, unsurprisingly, it was the Bridge Inn that hosted the official party celebrating the marriage of Edward, Prince of Wales to Alexandra of Denmark. It was reported that about 50 "of the respectable inhabitants of Newhaven attended and all had an enjoyable time", which they must have done as the dancing did not end until 4am.55

photo shows the Fort behind the parade.

Courtesy of Newhaven Museum

Chapter 5.
All At Sea.

Sailing ships of the 1830's appear to us in the twenty-first century to be far too small to sail the oceans of the world. Even compared to the smallest cargo ship of today they were small, just a few hundred tons, yet they covered thousands of miles. Sailing ships were the life blood of the nation, sailing both in coastal waters and internationally. Yet it was a most dangerous occupation with many reports of the loss of, not only the ships, but all those on board and sometimes just a few miles from and insight of a port.

In 1838, while travelling from a port at the mouth of the River Gambia in West Africa to London, the 150 ton Ocean was on the last leg of her journey when, at 2 am, she ran straight into the cliffs a mile or so from the Port of Newhaven at a place called Bearshide. Older maps show that Bearshide is on the sheer cliff face at what is now Peacehaven. Fortunately a coast-guard boatman heard the crash and sent word to his superiors, Lieutenant Franklin and, the Lloyds agent at Newhaven, Mr Cole.

The Ocean was carrying a cargo worth over £400 which, if it had not been for the swift action of the coast-guard and labourers supplied by Mr Cole, would have been lost. They also took command of the anchors and secured them so that the ship was saved from complete destruction. However, a dispute arose between the ship's owners and the rescuers over how much compensation should be paid for the rescue. Only £21 was offered and that was to be split between officers at 7 pounds and 7 shillings each with just 6 shillings for each labourer. (6 shilling is 30 p in modern coinage). However, Lloyds put in a claim for £50 which was subsequently refused by the ship's owners on the grounds that it was merely a labouring job.

A pre 1916 picture of Telscombe showing the area once known as Bears Hide. The buildings are the Coast Guard cottages, virtually all there was here then.

From the authors own post card collection

In the court, the judge said that the owners of ships should recompense those who put their lives at risk saving others and so awarded 50 guineas to the Lieutenants and 2 guineas to each of the labourers, including the boatman who spotted the ship.[56] A guinea was a term used for a coin worth one pound one shilling or £1.10. A sum of £2.20 would have been possibly about a week's wages for the labourers, far more than had been offered earlier.

≈≈≈≈≈≈≈≈≈

Captains of ships at sea are said to have had their wits about them and, in the days of sailing with no modern aids, they had a lot to think about. They had to be alert to danger and have the skills to understand the various sightings that were made, so as to ascertain the position of the craft. One would have thought that sobriety would have been important.

However, Nicholas Massey, the master of the schooner Sophia, died of drink in September 1838 whilst sailing from Cork to London. His body was brought ashore at Newhaven. Apparently, when they left Tenerife for Cork he drank a quarter of a 'pipe' of wine during the seven week voyage, which is about half a barrel or roughly 105 gallons. Therefore during the voyage he consumed something in the order of 26 gallons. His drinking continued, not even stopping on reaching Cork and remained inebriated or, as they said, "tipsy" for the 10 days they remained there.

Finally, while on board, it took two hands to keep him in bed and then when he came on deck he tried to jump overboard with his papers but was prevented. He finally died in his bed. As would be expected at the inquest, the Coroner recorded a verdict of "died from the effects of excessive drinking".[57]

≈≈≈≈≈≈≈≈≈

The coast between Rottingdean and Newhaven was always dangerous and there are many reports of ships going down there. One example was the total loss of the French vessel, the "Chasse Maree", which hit the rocks at Portabello at Telscombe Cliffs during a severe storm in early November 1838. All 20 persons on board were lost and the ship a "perfect wreck". There was only one reported body found and that was about 20 days later.[58]

≈≈≈≈≈≈≈≈≈

Prior to the Port of Newhaven taking over the cross channel ferry service, it used to run from Brighton, using Shoreham harbour. It was due to delays and contractual problems that Shoreham lost out to Newhaven. One of the paddle steamers on the old Shoreham-Dieppe route was the Dart owned by the General Steam Navigation Company. In October 1841 Captain Cheeseman sailed her out of Dieppe with 57 passengers bound for Brighton. However, a storm blew up over the channel and forced the Dart to return after 12 hours battling the waves. It was reported that 10 passengers disembarked at Dieppe, probably hoping to travel in better weather later.

Without the aid of weather forecasts, the captain felt he could try again but was caught in a storm again the next day. Having crossed the channel, the bad weather then forced him to seek refuge at Newhaven, his nearest harbour. Unfortunately, on entering the port, she hit the eastern piers which completely took out the paddle box and cook house. After sustaining such damage it was not possible to move her without carrying out major repair so a replacement ship had to be used in her place.[59] This incident took place before the port had been improved for safety and further high seas within the port caused more damage to the Dart before the repairs could be started.

≈≈≈≈≈≈≈≈≈

Major on-going improvements to the harbour were carried out throughout this period, both to stop the silting up and also so that it could take much larger vessels and cope with the intended cross channel steam packet service. From about 1845 improvements to Newhaven were discussed, with the intention that it should become a port of refuge for shipping in bad weather. Prior to this, in 1843, the 78 ton merchant ship, the "John and William", owned local man, Mr Catt of Bishopstone, was caught in a storm. The ship's captain found that, due to the poor state of the harbour, it could not be entered in these weather conditions. The ship, laden with barley, probably for his mill at Tide Mills, was a complete wreck with 2 hands being lost at sea.[60]

Tide Mills as it was in 1885. This large mill at Bishopstone (between Newhaven and Seaford). Both the mill and village have long gone.

Courtesy of Newhaven Museum

≈≈≈≈≈≈≈≈≈

There were some interesting trades related to the sea that have now virtually disappeared, one of which was the boulder collector. Boulders were large stones which the merchants sold to potteries mainly in Stoke-on-Trent where the Wedgewood factory among others were. In the 1860s Newhaven could boast at least 2 boulder merchants, George Cook and Charles Roberts, but it was the collectors who were the ones who put their lives at risk, as was the case in May 1847.

The bouldermen were still working in the early part of the twentieth century. Hence this picture of Tom Winder carrying a basket of boulders next to his sister Elizabeth, the picture dates form 1927.

Courtesy of Newhaven Museum

In May 1847 six boats were put to sea, as the weather was fine with only a light breeze. On board were some local labourers who were to collect the boulders. By eleven o'clock, the breeze had become a gale, forcing two boats belonging to W Stone and Son and Mr John Bull to be abandoned by the crew before being totally wrecked. The crews from these small ships were fortunately able to climb the cliff at Bearshide, which was shown on maps as the strip of coast situated between Friars Bay in Peacehaven and Portabello at Telscombe cliffs. Following earlier losses at sea, this dangerous piece of coast had been made into an escape route, a cut had been made into the rocks to allow men to climb to safety of the cliff top. Fortunately, one of the labourer's boats was able to be beached and saved while two more managed to return to the harbour.

The last boat's crew were not so lucky. Just as they reached the harbour they were struck by a large wave and sunk. Unfortunately, two of the five men on board went down with boat. Of the others, John Shepherd and Joseph Lower who, although swimmers, were dashed against the pier by the heavy sea and were not seen again. The last man held onto a plank and was saved at the last minute by Philip Mantle, who had a rope tied round his waist. With no weather forecast, even local knowledge was not always reliable.[61]

≈≈≈≈≈≈≈≈≈

Even by the late 1850s, with improvements having been made to the harbour, there were still the problems of reaching it. As previously mentioned, the coast was treacherous between Rottingdean and Newhaven. In particular, Portabello, which, today, is part of the sewerage outfall station of Southern Water, was not the place to be in a storm. During another terrible storm on 26 October 1859, on its way from Malaga to Leith, the Ariadne was driven on shore at Portabello and, although the crew were saved, the ship and all it's cargo were lost.[62]

≈≈≈≈≈≈≈≈≈

A couple of years later in 1862, another storm caused havoc at sea. This was still a time when whole families would live and work in very small sailing ships, earning a living by transporting goods round the coast. On board the 65 ton Bill Boy was 110 tons of Portland stone bound for London, together with a small two man crew was the ships master, his wife and six children. In the small hours of Friday morning 24 October 1862 she met a storm that caused her to spring a leak. The men worked continuously to pump water out but were slowly losing the battle with the water coming in.

As luck would have it, they were spotted by small fishing smack, the Wave, that realised the Billy Boy was in difficulties. Somehow, three men, including the Master, Mr Dorman, from the Wave were able to row a small boat to the Billy Boy. By the time they got on board they realised that there was nothing they could do to save her because of the damage sustained. The wife and small children were huddled below deck in three feet of water. The brave men managed to transfer everyone to the Wave. This was done just in time as, within five minutes of the last man being rescued, the Billy Boy went down. Being near Beachy Head, the master of the Wave headed for the shelter of Newhaven.

It was after nine o'clock that night, some hours after she sank, that the crew and family of the Billy Boy were welcomed at The Ark Inn by Mr Bull. The youngest of the six children was only six months old and some kind ladies of the town collected clothing and money for those rescued.[63] Those in distress at sea were always looked after by others connected to the sea.

Chapter 6
The new Lifeboat.

Newhaven has had a lifeboat since before the formation of the RNLI in 1824, with lifesaving at sea beginning there following the loss of the Brazen in 1800. A memorial to men lost when HMS Brazen when down can still be seen in the churchyard of St Michael's Church, with the loss of all but one of the 105 crew. Only a couple of days before, the 18 gun sloop had taken a prize ship off the coast of the Isle of White and sent a seven men over to crew that boat.[64] Again, it was in the area of Friars Bay that the HMS Brazen was caught in a storm and floundered. Three years later in 1803, one of the first ever lifeboats was stationed at Newhaven.[65]

There are some years when there is no record of a lifeboat being stationed there. One such period was during 1851, however, even without the aid of a lifesaving boat, a notable rescue was carried out by the local inhabitants which merited the award of the Royal Humane Society's medal. It was during the night of 31 January 1851, when a gale was blowing, that Mr Charles Cooke, the tide-waiter (customs officer who boarded incoming shipping to obtain customs duties), heard a cry for help. Without thinking, he took to a small boat and found that the Messrs Catt & Sons barge, the Integrity, had sunk in the river at Sleepers Hole. With the help of William Novis, Mr Cooke rescued the first three men, Aaron Elphick, George Smart and John Carter and got them into the boat. His small craft was then blown almost 30 yards off course, but he managed to get to the other side of the barge and rescue Thomas Tillman, who was clinging onto a couple of planks. Finally, he took all the rescued men to the watch house and gave them a restorative.[66] It was for this act of heroism that Mr Cooke was awarded the Royal Humane Society's medal. It was not noted if Mr Novis also received a similar award.

In late 1851 there were some initial reports that a lifeboat should be established in Newhaven. It was pointed out that there was no lifesaving vessel between Brighton and Eastbourne, and bearing in mind the number of boats and passengers who travelled from Newhaven to the continent, it was felt that a life boat should be situated there. At a meeting of the trustees of the Newhaven Harbour and Ouse Lower Navigation, Lt McKillop RN, who represented the Shipwrecked Fishermen and Mariners' Benevolent Society told the meeting that a lifeboat would cost about £125 and a boat-house a further £50. It was felt that if they re-used old materials the boat-house could be built for £20. After some further discussion the Trustees agreed to pay £30 towards a boat and build a boat-house.[67] The 'Friend in Need' was the first life boat to be housed in the new boat-house, it had 10 oars and 2 lugsails.[68]

Of all the lifeboats associated with Newhaven, only one seems to have come with any publicity. Lifeboats were donated by either individuals or groups of people, and many were handed over with a ceremony. The news of these was usually only reported locally. However, in 1877, one hand over was reported across the country. What made this boat of national interest was not because it was one of the largest self-righting lifeboats launched, at 37 feet, but that the funds raised came from the school children of the small Jewish community from all round the country.

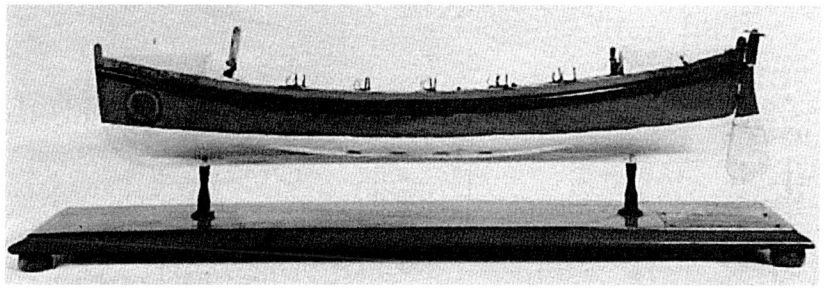

The Newhaven Museum only has a picture of a model of what was the original Michael Henry lifeboat would have looked like. This small rowing boat is all the volunteer lifeboat men had to rescue those who's ships were wrecked at sea near the town.

This photo was taken with kind permission of Newhaven Museum

In the 1870s the Jewish community was still relatively small, although well established. In 1875 the Jewish Scholars Lifeboat fund was started as an act of charity to support the work of the RNLI.[69] It had been started following a talk given by the editor of the Jewish Chronicle to a group of Jewish school children on the work of lifeboats. This was a man whose main purpose in life was to help everyone no matter what their religion was.[70] After his early death, this fund grew and was treated as his memorial. In conjunction with the RNLI, it was proposed that a new lifeboat paid for out of this fund should be stationed at Newhaven and named in his honour.

The boat was launched with great ceremony by the wife of Joseph Sebag, who was later to be knighted as Sir Joseph Sebag Montefiore, with Queen Victoria permitting him to adopt his uncle's surname of Montefiore. After the naming the boat "Michael Henry" it was handed over to Captain Jones on behalf of the Newhaven life-boat men. Following the handover the lifeboat crew rowed the boat up and down the river to the accompaniment of a band. This was followed by a luncheon that was held at the London and Paris Hotel followed by many speeches and toasts.[71]

≈≈≈≈≈≈≈≈≈

This was the start of a tradition which was to continue in 1897, when the Jewish community raised £700 for a second replacement lifeboat, also called Michael Henry. This boat was part of the diamond jubilee celebrations for Queen Victoria and was the cause of much celebration within the town. According to the reports, all the towns' dignitaries came, including representatives of both the British and French railways and ferry services along with most of the town's population. There was a procession round the town, followed by the ships in the harbour firing their guns in salute.[72]

Chapter 7
The flight of the King of France.

When Napoleon Bonaparte was defeated and the French republic was replaced by a monarchy, King Louis XVIII came to the thrown in 1814 and adopted the old form of absolute rule. For some years, what followed was a period of rebellion amongst the various political factions that made up the assembly selected by the King. On his death in 1824, his brother, Charles X, became king of France. Like his brother, he also tried to ignore the population and manipulate the parliament. By 1831 he was so unpopular that he was forced to abdicate and his cousin Louis-Philippe was offered the crown. To show he was more reformist, he took the title of King of the French People.

Some changes did take place but it was not enough and finally, in 1848, he and his family had to flee their country in disguise to save their lives. According to newspaper reports of the time, he and his wife took every precaution so as not to be recognised during their escape. Not only did they travel by night, reports state that "the King habiting himself in an old cloak and cap, having first shaved his whiskers, discarded his wig, and altogether disguised himself".[73] The King and Queen then made their way from the chateau at Dreux to Havre At times they pretended to be English and went so far as to have an interpreter to translate French to English. He chose to call himself Mr William Smith and carried a passport with that name on it.

A newspaper drawing of Louis Philippe with his family being helped ashore form a small rowing boat on arrival at Newhaven.

Courtesy of Illustrated London News (Iln.org.uk) - first published 11 March 1848

47

Eventually the party were able to board the steam packet Empress which made its way from the French coast to drop anchor just outside the harbour at Newhaven. According to some reports, it was the King himself who asked the ship to take them to Newhaven rather than the Empress's home port of Southampton, as he knew he would be welcomed there.[74] The ship's boat then carried one of the King's party into the harbour where arrangements were made at the Bridge Inn for an anonymous group of travellers to stay overnight. An envoy then carried on to London to made further arrangements for the exile of the King. With everything ready, an old gentleman and lady plus 4 attendants finally landed onto the safety of English soil.

Also from the Illustrated London News a drawing of the Royal party having breakfast at the Bridge Inn.

Courtesy of Illustrated London News (Iln.org.uk) - first published 11 March 1848

A horse and trap were ready to convey them to the Bridge Inn, but the owner of the trap, Mr Sims, could keep the secret no longer and said loudly "Welcome to England King Louis-Philippe! Welcome welcome!" By the time they had reached the Bridge Inn, the hostess Mrs Smith, had been made aware of who her important guests were. The seven members of the royal party were accommodated in six bedrooms and two sitting rooms, as well as an additional room for the attendants. Mr Catt of Bishopstone, who had been introduced to the King a couple of years earlier, was their first visitor, along with Mr Elphick and Mr Cole, all of whom offered their homes for the

Kings use. However, he decided to stay at the inn which was comfortable enough for them.

The King then wrote a letter to Queen Victoria, which was handed to the secretary of the Brighton Railway and Continental Steam Packet Company, Mr Irons. On leaving Newhaven, Mr Irons stopped at Lewes to ensure that a special train was made ready for the Royal party. He then continued his journey to London to hand the letter to the Queen. Meanwhile, the Royal party was given dinner by Mrs Smith, while ladies and gentlemen of the town provided clothing for the family. Finally, the following day they were able to board a special train to London.

The Bridge Hotel or Inn has always made a point of displaying its part in the escape and exile of the ex-king of France, Louis Philippe. This Victorian picture shows it as part of the hotels advertising.

Courtesy of Newhaven Museum

Chapter 8.
A Riotous Time.

Although normally a peaceful and industrious place, occasionally frustrations came to the surface that turned the calm town upside down. Although rare, this did happened a few times in Newhaven during this period. The reason was usually owing to some outside influence. Riotous behaviour was something that was a great worry to the Victorians and they had a clear definition of how it was defined and how to deal with it. Sometimes they would warn inhabitants by reading the Riot Act, in the hope that large groups of individuals would not gather together. It was the great fear of the upper and middle classes that law and order would break down as it had across the channel in France.

≈≈≈≈≈≈≈≈≈

1847.

Firework night could be difficult to police, with drink as well as fireworks and traditional fired tar barrels were the norm. This was a period when a lot of outside labour was camped nearby working on the railway and harbour. The town's counsellors were worried by this influx of navvies, so it was announced by the Town Crier that no fireworks were to be let off in the town's streets. Instead, permission was granted for those who wanted the usual celebration, that they should use Knowles Field for that purpose. Around eight o'clock at night, a man with a lighted tar barrel on his head was seen heading into town from Knowles Field, followed by about twenty others carrying large sticks. This worried and frightened the Parish Constable, William Baldwin. As the evening wore on, the numbers greatly increased as more people came into the town, even though they had been told not to.

As the proclamation had been read out be the Town Crier, a number of special constables had been sworn in, who were now called upon to stop any riot occurring in the town. According to the court reports, it appears that another lighted tar barrel had been brought into the town and was set down near the Bridge Inn. Using their authority, the constables tried to arrest Edward Adams as he put his barrel down. He claimed that those who had come into the town had not heard the declaration, as it had only been read in the town centre, meaning anyone on the Denton side of the river would not have heard it.

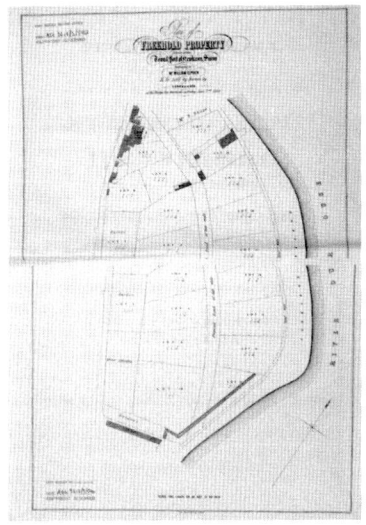

This 1860's map of the land known as The Knowles. The river is to the right with the town centre the grey shaded area towards the top left of the map.

Courtesy of The Keep ACC3412/3/590

At this point, one of the constables, John Pendrill, was struck on the head, possibly with one of the large sticks the crowd were carrying. Edward Adams was also hit at about the same time. To help the local police, Samuel Worsley, a constable employed by the railway, came to help. These "sticks", as the press called them, were about three feet long (about a meter) and as thick as a man's wrist. One of these weapons was held by William Millam, and was seen by Constable Samuel Worsley who, subsequently arrested him. The third person, John Welch, was also arrested and all of them were charged with riot. As there was not lockup or prison in Newhaven, the prisoners were held in the Bridge Inn. This action only inflamed the crowd outside and they then attacked the building, breaking a number of windows.

Although there was fighting between the police and the crowd on the night, it was the verdict of the court that it was not a riot. As those arrested had been working on the railway they would not have known anything about the proclamation made in the town about not assembling there. After the judge clearly informed the jury of what was meant, by the term riot and after careful consideration, the prisoners were cleared of the charges.[75]

≈≈≈≈≈≈≈≈

1851.

Another incident of riotous behaviour was linked to the railway and the navvies working on it. Some of the locals, especially the youngsters, felt that those outsiders engaged in building and maintaining the railway were not paying their way while the locals had to. From reading the reports, it does look as though the local young workers had a genuine grievance. It came down to the fact that in those days, to cross the river, there was a toll to pay at the bridge which was payable by everyone who was crossing it, even on foot.

During the period when the railway was being built, the navvies found this very expensive and inconvenient. With a little bit on ingenuity, they found their own way to avoid paying it. The problem as they saw it was the toll collector who was in their way and demanding money, therefore "one or two of the navvies to seize him and hold him fast, while the rest of the party passed across the bridge".[76] Though definitely not legal, this was rather an effective procedure and over time this became well known locally. It was not helped by the fact that the toll collector was rather an elderly gentleman.

Newhaven swing bridge was a toll bridge with the toll house on the right in front of the Tipper Brewery building.

Courtesy of Newhaven Museum

According to the newspapers, it seemed that, following the example of the navvies in the period up to 1847, many of the locals also demanded free passage across the bridge. After looking at their trust deed, the trustees of the bridge found that they were bound to charge a toll, however unpopular it was with the local community. There was one complication; the residents of Denton had been granted permission for free passage across the bridge. This had been granted by Mr Bates, the owner of the ferry, as part of the agreement for the building of the bridge. Naturally, this added to the grievances of the working men of Newhaven who did not live in the parish of Denton. It all came to a head in January 1851. The bridge had been in existence for over halve a century, so that the historic agreement made by the William Henry Bates, one of the major land owners of Denton, was well established.

Led by some of the workers from the shipyard, on a Monday night in January 1851, they gathered at the bridge to demand free access to cross so that they could go home. This was refused. At that point, some young men broke the gate with sledgehammers. Having been repaired in the meantime, the next night the mob returned and, again, were refused free crossing, so they attacked the gate once more.

By now some very worried trustees of the bridge were determined to put an end to this lawlessness. They checked their rights to the charging of a toll. Trustees Thomas Stone, William Stone and Mr Towner, stood their ground on the bridge. As it opened to let a cart through, the mob rushed the bridge and Mr Stone had his coat completely torn off his back.

Matters got out of hand and, as there was possibly only one policeman in Newhaven, additional police were brought in from another town under Superintendent Flanagan and Sergeant Akehurst. The Sussex Advertiser reported this riot, describing the men taking part as "Rebeccaites", (a little odd, as that was a term used for certain Welsh rioters who were dressed up as women in a period up to about 1844).[77] The same large group of men again appeared at the gate the following day but, on seeing a force of policemen, they did not attack it, though a few did risk personal injury by climbing over the gate which had now been reinforced with spikes. Luckily, this time, things calmed down a little after a while and the crowd disbursed.

To ensure that the trustees could still enforce the toll, they took out summonses against four of the shipyard apprentices who were seen taking part. Benjamin Woolgar, Alexander Woolgar, Edward Geering and Stephen Tucknott. These men were all taken to the Lewes Magistrates court and charged on counts of assault and taking part in a riot. These charges were exceedingly serious, but it was not the trustees intention to punish so much as to prove to everyone that a toll was payable. The reason that these men had been charged was that they all lived across the Ouse in Heighton and Bishopstone, about one and a half and three and half miles respectively from Newhaven and, more importantly, outside the Parish of Denton.

During the cross examinations the trustees could not prove that the defendants had actually torn Mr Stone's coat, which was brought in as an exhibit. Neither could they show that it was them who had held William Brooker, the toll collector. After much discussion between the parties and their solicitors they all came to a happy conclusion. The defendants apologised for their behaviour, promising not to do the same again. The prisoners were released and everyone agreed that it was only right and proper that the toll was charged.[78]

Unfortunately, a couple of days later Alexander Woolgar, egged on by his friends, tried to avoid the toll again and attacked Mr Brooker, who was aged about 75. He ended up in court once more and was rather fortunate that the court was lenient, as he could have ended up with months of imprisonment. Alexander was told that, in future, he must not break his word about paying the toll and should think before he acted. He was fined a little over a £1, including costs.[79] This was very lenient, as during that court session 187 people had been sent to prison, some with hard labour.

≈≈≈≈≈≈≈≈≈

1866.

A few years later, when the harbour was being improved again, there was a shortage of men to do the heavy labouring work. These men were known as navvies, which is short for navigators. Foreign workers were brought in which was unpopular with locals, who thought that they were taking work away from them. In 1866 there were a number of riots caused by too many foreign labourers being employed. Some of the disturbances arose because the local population thought that the outsiders were being paid rates different to them. According to some newspapers, there was talk that the Belgian workers who had been brought in were earning less than the English and this caused resentment. Serious fighting broke out at a railway project on the Kent and Sussex border. Subsequently, many of the antagonists appeared in various courts in both counties. [80]

In 1866, there were only two policemen in Newhaven and the question of the need for more police in the town was raised, following violent incidents which had caused disruption to law and order in the town. What we may consider a heavy handed approach was sometimes taken with small incidents as, at that time, there was little understanding to the causes of social unrest. Even small isolated incidents of criminal behaviour would end with the word riot being used both in court and in the papers. Even if this word was not used, any violence was treated very harshly.

The Blue Anchor was a public house with a reputation for fights. It was situated in the High Street and was later a green grocers.

Courtesy of Newhaven Museum

For example, in mid July 1866, a navvy called Charles Brown was drunk at the Blue Anchor and the landlord's wife him asked to leave. He refused and assaulted her. He was charged with being drunk and riotous behaviour and was fined 17s 9d, which he could not pay, so spent 10 days in prison.[81] During the same week, four men working on the new bridge at Newhaven were involved in two separate fights over their sacking. They were charged with assault but failed to turn up in court so PC Osborne was called upon to arrest them. Initially, only George Climpson could be found and brought before the magistrates. He was found guilty and, because he had absconded, his fine was £1 15s. At the same court two navvies were charged with sleeping rough in Mr Willard's hay stack. Found guilty of this very serious charge they were sentenced to seven days hard labour. [82]

More seriously, there was a battle between navvies and the police on the 22 August 1866. A usual Saturday night's drinking ended when the Bridge Hotel required the police to help eject a number of navvies who were causing a disturbance there. A couple of hours later, at about 1 am on the Sunday morning, Constables Osborne and Moore came across the same group of navvies fighting and causing a disturbance. The constables decided that they had to break the crowd up and disburse them. Looking for a ring leader, Constable Osborne took hold of one of the men, while PC Moore tried to stop the others helping the prisoner. At this point the navvies turned on the police to rescue their man. During the fight that ensued, a man called Soap attacked PC Moore with a bat, knocking him unconscious.

By the time PC Osborne reached his colleague, PC Moore had a broken nose and had almost lost an eye. Now being kicked to the ground, PC Osborne found it was impossible keep hold of the prisoner, so released him. He and other four men ran away, to what they hoped would be, freedom. Quickly PC Osborne obtained the use of a trap to take his stricken friend to Lewes, where his father was keeper of the Vagrants Ward. After leaving him there, he went on to get help from Sergeant Peacock and Superintendent Jenner, who got a number of constables together and chased after the navvies.

By eight o'clock in the morning, the navvies gave themselves up to the police without resistance in Rottingdean, as they realised that there was no point in fighting the officers sent to arrest them. From Rottingdean they were taken to Lewes Police court, where they were brought before the local magistrate. The papers described them as "strong, burly-looking men", indicating their guilt. In the court, Mr Soap's bloody clothes were shown to prove he had attacked the policeman. In the end, Soap and his associates were sentenced to hard labour for periods between three and eight months.

Because of the risk of further riot in Newhaven, Sergeant Peacock and two other constables were dispatched to Newhaven to help keep order. With the extra police in the town further trouble was avoided.[83]

≈≈≈≈≈≈≈≈≈

1876.

In May there was a riot that, as one paper said, caused much excitement in the town. It was a fight between soldiers and sailors from the army based at the Fort and the ships moored in the harbour. On the Saturday night a number of the soldiers from the Royal Artillery fought a running battle with sailors based in the port. The fight involved not only using fists to punch and feet to kick each other, but also bats, which caused number of men to be seriously hurt. It started at about 9 pm, when there had been just a small argument between an artilleryman and a sailor called Winter in the pub, which appeared to end when they left.

A couple of hours later, about a dozen artillerymen entered the Blue Anchor and were followed by Winter who, for some reason, wanted to start a fight with these men who were due to leave town that week. Either he or a friend of his threw a tumbler, which cut open the head of one of the soldiers, hospitalising him. This time the police were called upon to evict them.

Newhaven Fort is behind the sailing boat in this picture from this very early 1900's postcard.

From the authors own collection.

Word spread rapidly and, within a very short time, a large group of between 20 to 30 soldiers and sailors had gathered in the High Street near the pub. The soldiers were outnumbered by sailors who fought them some of the way back to the barracks at the Fort. According to the police evidence, a few of the soldiers used the fencing ripped up from around Mr Stone's property in Meeching Road to defend themselves. It was the sailors who were charged by the police and appeared in the dock on the Tuesday morning. Walter Lower was fined £1 for being disorderly and refusing to leave the Blue Anchor when asked to do so by the landlord, John Jeffries. Next to appear were John Manser, Henry Richardson, James Bryant and Henry Pettitt, who were all charged with being drunk and disorderly by the police. This case was brought by police sergeant Renville and police constable Whapham, who were able to show that these four were the ringleaders and were so drunk that they did not know what they were doing. These sailors were each fined 30s (£1.50) and were warned that they would be severely dealt with if they appeared in court again. Finally in court that day, George Winter and Edward Eager were found guilty of riotous behaviour and were both fined £1, including costs.

The anger of the soldiers at being put down and beaten by sailors was just too much for some of them. On the Monday night, gunners from the Royal artillery, 6th battery 3rd brigade who were stationed at Newhaven Fort, came into the Blue Anchor looking for trouble. With between 20 and 30 gunners entering the bar the 4 or 5 sailors quickly left, not wanting a fight this time. Seeing the sailors leave, one of the soldiers, John Wilson, said "if there are no sailors let's settle the ... landlord".

The soldiers began to cause a riot inside the Blue Anchor, it starting with one of them smashing a 14 inch iron bolt down onto the counter of the bar breaking it. Then the rest of them started to throw the glasses about, the force of which embedded glass in the walls. To protect himself, the landlord picked up an unloaded gun and threatened to shoot the next man who threw a glass. While he went out the back to get the police, more of the pub was smashed up. Finally the police assembled outside and Major Anderson, the men's commanding officer, called the men to fall in outside. This time the militiamen were brought before the court and four of them ended up with six weeks hard labour.[84]

Chapter 9.
A murder most horrid.

Crimes of murder enthralled the Victorians as much as they do us today. Although not glamorised, it appears that the newspapers enjoyed a good murder, going by the headlines they used, though this was possibly just their way of increasing their circulation. They were all very graphic in detail, far more so than any editor today would dream of printing. Violence was depicted to show just how dangerous the lowers classes of society, especially the criminal classes, were.

This was also a period when violence against women was accepted as the norm, provided it was inflicted by the husband, and within strict limits.[85] These limits were often imposed by neighbours, who would reprimand the husband who was too violent, stepping in to protect the wife or give her refuge for a short period. The murder of a husband was treated as a much more serious offence than that of a husband murdering his wife. He would still have to face the courts but could get a more lenient sentence by being accused of manslaughter rather than murder, which carried the death sentence.

Although generally a peaceable place sometimes that peace was broken, as has already been noted, by the violence of a small group. There were the rare occasions when your neighbour did not act expected, with the shock of them committing murder. During this period there was an acceptable level of violence within the home and workplace but anything more was treated as a crime. As the Victorians seemed to take an interest in the blood and violence that came with murder, therefore the following reports are slightly toned down for today's public.

≈≈≈≈≈≈≈≈

1830.

Newhaven, although not known for murder, has had the odd isolated experience of this type of crime. When a brutal murder occurred, such as the one in 1830, it was reported in virtually every newspaper of the day. This may have been both because of the nature of the crime and the fact that the husband admitted killing his wife immediately. By any standard it was a brutal attack. Harry Winter, the captain and part owner of a trading vessel the Gage, had used the fire-shovel to batter his wife to death on the night of Friday 8th October 1830.

The next day an inquest was held at the Bridge Inn in Newhaven before the coroner, Mr Gell, and, what the papers called, "a most respectable jury". It was reported that Ann and Harry Winter had "lived unhappily together", with reports of many quarrels. There had been an argument in the morning before he set sail for Lewes and he did not return home until about nine o'clock the same night in a state of intoxication. The inquest heard from various witnesses as to what happened early the following morning.

A view along the River Ouse looking at the ship yards somewhere in this area the murder would have taken place.

Courtesy of Newhaven Museum

The newspaper reports stated that, Sarah Lower, who lived near the ship-yard, had passed the Winter's house about ten o'clock on Friday night and heard raised voices. She asked a passing labourer, Mr William Mantell, to go up to the house but he declined, not wanting to get involved so she threw some pebbles at the window. Hearing a table fall over, both went on their separate ways. Early the following morning, Harry Winter went across the road to call on his near neighbour, Mrs Dyer. Asking if his wife had any broken bones, Harry just said "he was afraid it was worse than that". On her way to Mr Winter's house she passed Mrs Stone's house where her daughter, Ann, had been staying. Both mother and daughter then went to the house. On seeing blood on the door step, Sarah Dyer refused to go in so Ann went in and found the battered and bloodied body of Mrs Winter.

During the morning the two local surgeons, John Bissett and Mr Charles Verrall, examined the virtually naked body of Ann Winter and both reported the injuries she had sustained to the jury. These must have been considerable, as the shovel and poker were both bent and bloodied. The inquest jury immediately found Harry Winter guilty of murder and he was sent to Horsham prison to await trial at the next Assizes.[86]

At his trial on 24th December 1830, further facts came out in court. There were a couple of versions of what happened that were described in court, but in the end the full story of both the dreadful murder and their everyday lives comes out. Harry Winter had been married to his wife for over 30 years and, during that time, they had shared the life of seafarers together. It was reported that, on at least three occasions in the past, they had been shipwrecked together. Even though they must have had their ups and downs, they loved each other enough to stay together all that time. About a year and a half previous to the murder, they had taken a house in Newhaven and settled down. It was also noted that in recent months they had both started to drink heavily which was the cause of arguments between them. However on the day of the murder Harry had bought some gift items for his wife, while in Lewes.

On Friday 8th November at about 9pm, Mr Winter returned to Newhaven and went to the Bridge Inn for a glass of grog and a glass of brandy. At about 10 o'clock he left the Inn and went home, assuring the landlord that he would comfort his wife. It was shortly afterwards that Sarah Lower heard raised voices in the Winter household and threw the stones at the window to stop them arguing. Then shortly after Mr Mantel, who was lodging at the Ship Inn confirmed that he saw Mr Winter strike his wife through the window, with the aid of a candle which was still alight in the room. No comment was passed on to Mr Mantel continuing to his lodgings and not taking any action. This may well be because beating a wife was acceptable but murder was not.

At around 2am the following morning two, bargemen, William King and William Ellis, were guiding their barge past the Winters' house, when they saw a man and woman on the river bank. The woman was kneeling and appeared naked while the man seemed to have just a shirt on. They saw the woman struck by the man and fall. Ellis heard the woman cry "murder" and "Oh, forgive me this time". When they were about thirty yards away, one of the men did call out but Mr

Winter took no notice so they carried on. As previously mentioned, a certain amount of violence was accepted. These bargemen saw a lot of wives being "chastised" by husbands, especially amongst the lowers classes who lived by the river.

In the morning Ann Dyer was at the house of Edward Stone when her mother came in with Mr Winter. Mrs Dyer asked her daughter to accompany them to Mrs Winter's house. Leaving her mother outside and seeing blood on the steps Ann Dyer went inside to the front room with Mr Winter. She said "you cruel man, what have you done?" to which he replied "I have killed my wife. I shall be hung for it. I hope I shall." Ann then went into the bedroom and saw Mrs Winter lying dead on the floor with her hand over her bloodied her left ear and bruises and blood on her face. All she had on were her stockings and part of her chemise, which was torn and also covered in blood.

The next witness was Thomas Carter, who saw Mr Winter in the morning and reported that he said "Captain what's the matter?" To which Winter replied "She has torn the shirt of my back, and I have taken the gown off her back" Thomas then asked "Captain do you mean she is dead?" He was followed into the dock by the police; firstly James Washington, a constable, produced the torn and blooded shirt. Then constable Thomas Egles identified the poker and shovel.

Finally the two local doctors were called to give their evidence. This consisted of graphic accounts of the wounds Mrs Winter received.

Rather than speak at his trial a written statement by Mr Winter was read out, in which he stated that he could not believe what he had done to the wife he loved. He went on to explain that he loved his wife and had even bought her a new pair of spectacles in Lewes along with a fowl for their dinner. It was the drink that was the problem. His wife was drunk and he was not sober when he got home and had no recollection of what had happened later that evening.

Following the judge's summing up it was concluded that the murder was caused by both the husband and wife being intoxicated. After just 10 minutes, the jury found Harry Winter guilty of manslaughter. He was then sentenced to transportation for life.[87]

≈≈≈≈≈≈≈≈≈

1881.

Newhaven is bordered by Piddinghoe to the west, Denton to the north and Seaford to the east and it is just over the town boundary to Piddinghoe that we now turn. It was in August 1881 that James Diplock of Piddinghoe was charged with the murder of his wife. The village had a very small population of just 225 people in 46 houses, so was a close knit community. It was not uncommon for locals to walk between the village and Newhaven for both work and food and drink.

As previously mentioned, violence towards a wife was common, although getting less so by this time. Also, drink was cheap and plentiful, particularly as alcohol was safer to drink than water. As with the murder of Ann Winter, drunkenness was again at the heart of the story.

When Emily Diplock died on the 22nd July 1881, her death was treated as accidental by the Coroner. This may have been because James Diplock, an agricultural labourer, had formerly been a member of Brighton Police force. Therefore, when he stated that his wife had fallen downstairs it was taken as the truth. When she was initially admitted as a patient with a fractured skull, the hospital was told that, having arrived home a little drunk, Emily had fallen downstairs. Her husband, thinking she was not hurt, left her there and went to bed. As she was still on the floor at the bottom of the stairs in the morning and apparently injured, he asked a neighbour to get the doctor from Newhaven. Even at this time, the hospital surgeon who carried out the post mortem did not raise any questions and accepted the story of the fall, even with all the injuries.

To our eyes it already seams suspicious but this was a rural community in the late nineteenth century. After the inquest Mr Diplock disappeared with his seven year old daughter. It was only then that the neighbours began to talk about his cruelty. This prompted the police to commence their investigations and the extent of the violence inflicted by him on his wife became apparent, as well as their drunkenness, which was also highlighted.

On the 19th August 1881, a month after his wife's death, James Diplock appeared in the magistrate's court charged with murder, having been arrested in Shoreham, where he was working on a farm. It was reported that he appeared in the dock with his young daughter.

The initial story seems unclear but at about 3pm on Saturday afternoon Emily Diplock asked her neighbour at Lodge Farm (just over a mile or 1.8m from Piddinghoe), Elizabeth Akehurst, to look after her front door key. Elizabeth then saw Emily walk off in the direction of Piddinghoe village. This was confirmed by George Akehurst, who saw the Diplocks in the Royal Oak beerhouse, but not together, at about 9pm that night. They were both drunk. It was not until about 9.30 the following morning that they were seen again, when Elizabeth helped undress Emily after James and a man by the name of Backshall got her upstairs in her own home.

Piddinghoe the the Royal Oak an 1870's picture

Courtesy of Newhaven Museum.

The Royal Oak Beerhouse, sometimes called Berries after the landlord James Berry, was quite full of couples who lived nearby, all of whom would have left to walk home within about half an hour of each other. According to a number of witnesses, as the Diplocks wandered home, they were arguing about money, including the matter of Emily spending all James's money on drink. A short while later, while walking along a farm track, James Diplock was seen hitting and kicking his wife but no one worried about this. One witness even heard James tell her to get up and, when she refused, saw him kick her. This does not fit in with what was the seen as a general lessening of violence towards wives in the latter part of the nineteenth century but, being a small, tight knit community, James Diplock's violence was taken for granted. [88]

The following morning a local farmer saw Emily on the ground but took no notice. Someone else spotted a woman lying on the ground, though it was not stated who, his thought was that she "ought not to lie out in the sun". It was only later that Thomas Godden, with the help of Stephen Adams and William Blackshall, collected her in a wheelbarrow covered with a sack. When they arrived at the hill to pick her up, they found she was badly bruised and bleeding, with torn clothing. Back at home Elizabeth Akehurst helped undress Emily and put her to bed. Emily was badly bruised and her face swollen and kept asking for beer and brandy.

This was one of the headline pictures in the Illustrated Police News on 27th August 1881. It is the artists impression of Emily Diplock being taken home on the wheelbarrow.

Courtesy of British Library Board ©

At the trial in November the judge, Lord Coleridge, asked why both the Akehurst's had lied in the Coroners Court, knowing that Emily had not fallen down stairs. Mr Akehurst simply stated that no man was obliged to criminate himself. The judge reminded him that that was exactly what he was doing. Mr Akehurst also stated that he only repeated what the surgeon had told him to say. At that point, the judge sent Mr and Mrs Akehurst away with a caution for lying.

The local surgeon, Thomas Cann of Newhaven, saw Mrs Diplock on the Sunday and noticed her bruising. Mr Diplock simply said that he had smacked her in the mouth, which was all part of the lie. It was not until the Wednesday that the Doctor advised that she be taken to the hospital in Brighton, where she died 2 days later. The house surgeon told the court that it was injuries to the brain that caused death and that the other injuries could have been caused by a fall, though he could not be sure.

In his summing up, Lord Coleridge told the jury that he noted that the prisoner had used more violence than he intended, which could mean it was not premeditated. In the end this was the jury's view as well. James Diplock was found guilty of manslaughter and given a sentence of penal servitude for life; the most severe punishment for a crime which was virtually murder.[89]

≈≈≈≈≈≈≈≈

1893.

The Bridge Hotel in Newhaven was one of the venues where coroners held inquests for deaths in the local area. On the Downs just above Newhaven a woman called Emily Twiggs was found brutally murdered. It took a few days to discover who she was but then, with remarkable speed, the police were quickly able to charge someone with the crime. A few of the early reports gave the wrong name of the deceased, until her nephew came forward and was able to identify her; "she comes from a good family, but about two years ago gave way to loose habits and had not been home since. Her name was Emily Twiggs, and her husband (her second) still alive." From this it was clear to the Victorian reader exactly what sort of woman she had turned out to be.

On the front page of The Illustrated Police News was this drawing that put Newhaven on the map.

Courtesy of British Library Board ©

Looking down Bridge Street from South Road towards the High Street. Taken in 2012

Newhaven Swing bridge with Denton Island to the left. Taken 2014

It is possible that this is the view the Victorians would have had, the back of Chapel Street as it is in 2012

Newhaven High Street from the Bridge Hotel as it was in 2012

Meeching Court today is the site of the former Meeching Court Farm as it is in 2012

Newhaven High Street in 2012 from Brighton Road to the Bridge Hotel.

In 2012 this is the Hope Inn in days gone by it was next to another pub, the Sea Houses

The building in front of us was the site of the original Barclays Bank, next door to The White Hart. Taken in 2012

A photo taken in 2013 of the memorial to the crew of HMS Brazen in the churchyard of St Michael's

The Flying Fish at Denton, now opposite a housing estate which was not there in 1890's.

Taken in 2014

In 1866 there was the story of the "elopement in humble life" they would have walked down this road through Piddinghoe, the main C7 road now is to our right this in now just the road to the village.

Taken in 204

The tradition of shipbuilding and repairing still continues in Newhaven in the Robinson Road area.

Taken in 2014

In early April 1883, Emily's body was found on the Canter Hill, Denton, near Newhaven. Aged 45, it was very clear just how far she had fallen. It was reported that her father John Saunders owned property in Saltash, Cornwall, known as Slade Park. Her first husband, Mr Bishop, was an usher and her second was Mr Potts, a butcher, whom she had left about four years previously. Recently it had been reported that she was of no fixed abode and was living with Job Taylor, a hawker aged 35. From a good middle class background, she had fallen so low that she was now virtually a member of the criminal classes.

Although the murder took place on Tuesday 5th April, it was not until the report on the 22nd April that full story emerged. Henry Webber, the farmer, found the body of a woman covered with some bagging, part of which he removed and saw her battered face. The next witness at the hearing was Alfred Goldey, a labourer from Crowborough, who knew the couple as Mary and Job Taylor husband and wife. On the Monday night, after the three of them had been travelling the county, they ended up sleeping on Canter Hill till the morning. The next morning Alfred walked into Newhaven to look for work for himself and met the couple that afternoon in the Jolly Sailor before they all moved on to the Railway Inn. By the time they left the Railway Inn, Emily, or Mary as she was now known, was quite drunk and arguing with Job.

The Three Corners at Denton, with the Flying Fish in the centre of the picture.

Courtesy of Newhaven Museum

Back on the hill Job tore her jacket, saying he had given her enough and she was always drunk. A little while later they walked the mile or so back at the Flying Fish in Denton, where Alfred bought some beer for them, as Mary was too drunk to go in, as was, probably, Job. At some point after that Alfred left them. He knew Mary was too drunk to go any further. The sacking covering Emily's body was identified as belonging to Job and he was convicted of murder. Although, later at the assizes, this was commuted to manslaughter with fourteen years penal servitude. [90]

The Flying Fish at Denton about a mile and half from Newhaven.

Courtesy of Newhaven Museum

Chapter 10
Other crimes or not!

Victorian crime often seems much more brutal and sensational than that which we see every day on the television news. It was also a period when the punishment was very severe and far beyond anything that would be handed down by the courts today. In saying this, however, there were occasions when the court would dismiss a case that would have, under normal circumstances, ended with a severe punishment. Overall, the area of Newhaven had not had too many crimes reported in the Victorian newspapers. Those that are included here range from the minor to the very serious, although this was an era when crime was sometimes seen differently. During the Victorian period the punishment passed on the convicted criminal was to change, as were certain attitudes to what was seen as a crime.

≈≈≈≈≈≈≈≈≈

1839.

Shopkeepers lived on the premises, often with the shop forming part of their house. During the night of 5th February 1839, a robbery took place at the shop of Mr William Stone. The intruders entered through the parlour of the house via the window which although it had been shuttered the burglar forced open before breaking the glass. The robbery was noticed at about 5 am, when Mr Wilder, an employee of Mr Catt, was going to work. He saw that the shutters were open and that the parlour window was held open by a dessert knife. On seeing this he woke the household who then found that they had been robbed.

Once inside the house they were able to force the inner shop door open. The intruders then took a quantity of shawls, waistcoats, Irish linen and silk, as well as some money and a decanter containing ginger wine. Possibly hearing a sound, the burglars left in a hurry. A reward of £20 for the capture of the thieves was offered, indicating the value of the goods stolen.[91] It was found later that Mr Muggridge had also been robbed of some joints of meat the same day.

≈≈≈≈≈≈≈≈≈

1855.

On 6th March a former policemen, now a labourer, was charged with assaulting the police. As with many of the cases reported, the defendant had been drinking, which he claimed caused him to act out of character. Thomas Winder was seen fighting another man when Constable John Peerless saw that they were causing a disturbance and attempted to break it up. It was a brave move by PC Peerless as Mr Winder got hold of his collar and told him that it was not police business to stop them as it was a fair stand-up fight. With all the shouting that ensued, a further five or six men joined in the fight. When brought before the magistrates, Thomas Winder apologised, saying that he had drunk too much at a ship launch party. This did not help, as the magistrate pointed out he had been a policemen and so should have known better. He was fined 10s with 15s costs (the equivalent of £1.15 in total).[92]

Under the heading of "troublesome wife" in the court reports of Monday 16th July 1855, was the case of Ellen Dooley. She was drunk and went to find her husband, who was a stoker at the gas works. When she found him, Ellen created such a scene by abusing her husband that is was necessary to call for the aid of the police. PC Peerless arrived and, after remonstrating for some time with her to calm her down and go home, he ended up having to arrest Mrs Dooley and taking her into custody. Not only was this embarrassing for Mr Dooley but, as the magistrate said, he would also have to pay his wife's fine of 15s as well as keep her from making such a scene again.[93]

Another domestic dispute was brought before the courts in August of the same year. The chairman of the bench initially told the couple to go away and resolve their dispute themselves, but the parties refused. By chance, although not related, the neighbours both had the same surname, Stace. There was Mary Ann and her husband Samuel, who lived next door to Benjamin Stace together with the rest of his family whose names were not included in the news article.

The case brought before the court was that of assault which was brought by Mary Ann against her next door neighbour, Benjamin. It started when Mary was drying her husband's clothes on his return from a fishing trip. After taking his boots off, Samuel threw the water in his boots over the wall. Water landed on his neighbour, who was sitting on the step of his house. This so angered Benjamin that he hit Mary. He and his father then followed them into their house and struck Samuel too. This was disputed by Benjamin, who said he was hit by Mary with the boot and her husband then hit him also. This case ended as it had begun, with the court dismissing the case as they needed to resolve matters between themselves.[94]

≈≈≈≈≈≈≈≈

1856.

Some robberies were considered very serious and the punishment given was harsh. However, with no welfare state, it was hard to feed a family if you were poorly paid so crime was occasionally worth the risk. On 9th January, George Lower, a carrier from Denton, was taking a couple of hams from Mr Stone in Newhaven to William Woolgar's shop in Seaford. It was early evening so he rested his horse at the Railway Inn while he took some refreshment. In the end he stayed for two hours. The hams were left on the back of the cart, though it was not mentioned if they were covered or not.

When he finally got to Seaford there was only one ham on the cart. This was another job for PC Pearless to investigate. George remembered seeing James Simmons, a fireman on the Dieppe steamer, in the Railway Inn earlier. Enquiries found that, on returning to his ship, James fried some ham. He had told a fellow fireman on the same steamer that, with just 8d, he had bought 1½lbs of ham at 9d per pound. However, he told another fireman he told the cost was 9½d per pound. PC Pearless, checking Mr Simmons locker, found a piece of ham which he took away for identification, after being told it had been bought for 10d per pound.

Although neither Mr Woolgar nor William Stone could positively identify the ham, they were sure it was similar to the hams sold by them. James Simmons was found guilty and sentenced to 6 months hard labour.[95]

PC Peerless was again called into action in May 1856, when he arrested a pauper living in the Newhaven Workhouse and charged him with stealing spoons. The case arose after Mary Hope, the servant of Mrs Susannah Gray, found that a spoon was missing after the ash man, Richard Gantling, had been. The spoon, worth about 4s, (about 20p) was valuable and had the initials J.S.G. engraved on it. Mary Hope heard that the spoon was with Richard Gantling in the Newhaven Union House, and informed PC Peerless.

Having been searched by PC Peerless, Richard claimed that he had found it. The governor of the House said that the prisoner had always behaved well and that Mrs Gray had asked the court not to be too severe with him. The court took this into account and he only had to serve one month's hard labour.[96]

≈≈≈≈≈≈≈≈≈

1862.

In 1862 an interesting case came before the courts which was somewhat different from the norm. Although it was a charge of theft, it was theft itself that was in dispute. Richard Hoare, a ship and property owner, was charged in August 1862 with stealing a Japanese cabinet worth £50 from William Bütner. He was also charged with receiving the cabinet knowing it to be stolen.

The facts of the case are, as the newspaper stated, rather peculiar. On 17 May 1862, the Dutch ship the Resident Von Son was wrecked between Seaford and Newhaven. The Coast-guard saved captain Bütner and his crew, along with most of the cargo. The Dutch consul, Mr Vandenburg, came to Newhaven and arranged for the cargo to be stored in the Newhaven warehouse belonging to Mr Hoare. Mr Hoare was told that no item was to be removed from his warehouse until the ship's owners and underwriters gave permission. Included amongst the items stored was a cabinet purchased by Captain Bütner in Japan as a present for his wife.

Later, when the goods were inspected, the cabinet was missing, though the Captain was sure it had been taken from his ship to the warehouse. However, in June, Mr Vandenburg happened to visit Mr Hoare's house and saw cabinet that looked very similar to the one he knew had been lost. He asked where it had come from and Richard Hoare said he bought it from a man in the street and that it was, in fact, only made of papier mâché. The consul was suspicious and, after discussing it with Mr Bütner, showed him a rough sketch of the cabinet. On seeing the sketch Mr Bütner confronted Mr Hoare who said he hoped he would not be prosecuted over it.

It now appeared that the two men did not get on and an action for defamation was taken out by Richard Hoarexe against Captain Bütner. It was only following that action in court that the present case was brought. The court was informed that no attempt had been made to hide the cabinet which was in the parlour of Mr Hoare's house.

The jury quickly found Mr Hoare not guilty, to which those in the public gallery applauded.[97] At this time, juries would hardly discuss the case before agreeing the verdict, so the speed of a decision was not unusual. Also, the fact that the defendant was a man of standing in the community and the accuser was a foreigner did not help the plaintiff's case.

≈≈≈≈≈≈≈≈

1864.

In another pub fight that ended with a man going to prison, Richard Belton was charged with assaulting Alexander Winder and occasioning actual bodily harm. On 29th May, Winder and William Noakes were in the Engineers Arms, a beerhouse or, as we know it, a pub, when Richard Belton came in and immediately started to insult Alexander. Some strange facts came out, for example, Richard Belton, a sailor in the Naval Reserve, had recently been accused of stealing a duck. When Richard pulled a knife, the landlord intervened and the knife put away. After a drink, Alexander sang a song.

The Engineers Arms public house in Railway Road Newhaven.

Courtesy of Newhaven Museum

Mr Winder left the pub a little before 10 pm, followed shortly by Mr Belton, his mother and as few others. A short distance along the road, Richard Belton again drew his knife and, this time, cut Mr Winder's coat before stabbing him in the hand. The wound was so bad that Dr Noakes was called to dress it. He said that the hand would not be able to be used for some weeks. Although at the assize hearing Richard Belton contradicted the evidence of Alexander Winder, the case was proved. Richard had to serve eight months with hard labour.[98]

≈≈≈≈≈≈≈≈≈

1866.

A crime may not always take place but the parties still may have gone to court to see if they could prove their case. Such a case was entitled "An elopement in low life" in one paper and "An elopement in humble life" in another. The case was that of William Pratt, who was charged with stealing a basket, a cotton shirt and a key; goods to the value of 2s 9d. William Pratt and a fellow lodger were brickmakers who worked for and lived in the house of George Reed and his wife. It was known that the Reed's was not a happy marriage. On the afternoon of Saturday 31st March 1866, the Mrs Reed left the house by the front door. Just a few minutes later, the lodgers left by the back door.

Mrs Reed was somewhat enamoured by the young men living in her house and had started to borrow money for them. She was using her husband's credit without his permission and this cause a number of rows. The young men claimed they left with her on this occasion to protect her from her husband.

George Reed was not immediately suspicious but, when he noticed the men's caps and his wife's shawl missing, he checked further and found sheets and blankets missing as well. After checking at the railway station he called on PC Osbon to investigate. PC Osbon and Mr Reed decided to follow the road to Lewes by horse and cart and, just before Iford, they came upon Mr Pratt and Mrs Reed arm in arm. Mr Reed identified articles mentioned in the charge sheet in the basket which William Pratt was holding. However, at the court hearing it was found that, as the couple had been stopped from eloping, no crime had been committed, so Mr Pratt was discharged. It was not mentioned if Mr and Mrs Reed lived together again![99]

≈≈≈≈≈≈≈≈≈

1878.

Life in the workhouse was just too much for James Ling, and he rebelled in the only way he knew how. He was charged with the crime of tearing up his shirt and trousers while on the casual ward of the Newhaven Workhouse.[100] At the end of the court hearing he was sent to prison for a month with hard labour.

≈≈≈≈≈≈≈≈≈

1879.

One of those who were paid to help others but decided, in this case to help himself, was Albert Brooker. Employed as a relieving officer to Newhaven Union, Albert used his position to obtain money by forging receipts and so take money from the Board of Guardians. In court in 1879, he was charged with forgery and obtaining money by false pretences. For some time, he had taken money meant for paying the union's bills and wrote out false receipts which he handed to the board. In addition, he kept the 2s 6d per week meant for a poor widow for himself, although he included the payment in his books. He was sentenced to twelve months imprisonment.[101]

≈≈≈≈≈≈≈≈≈

1890.

Smuggling was part and parcel of life in a coastal town and the Customs Officers were employed to ensure that duty was paid when required. The ways items can be smuggled into the country are various, but perhaps the most audacious recorded was in October 1890. Lord Salisbury was the Prime Minister and, on 9th October 1890, he and his household were returning from France and, naturally, arrived at Newhaven.

It was, however, in the unexpected inspection of his lordship's carriage that the customs officers discovered several gallons of brandy and spirits as well as a considerable number of cigars. The coachman was detained by the police. However, this was the early part of the story and, as the newspaper stated, it could have been any other member of the household who attempted to smuggle these goods into the country.

Whichever member of the Prime Minister's household thought they could get away without paying the duty, they did not realise that, no matter of your status, the customs men could still check passenger's baggage. No record was made of His Lordship's reaction to this incident.102

≈≈≈≈≈≈≈≈≈

1891.

Mr Marshall Hall was one of the most eminent and famous barristers of his day and was born in Brighton. Prior to becoming, what some called, "the great defender", in one of his early cases he represented Miss Rose Banks in a breach of promise case. At this time, a woman could sue a man to whom she was engaged to be married if he broke the engagement without good reason.

St Michael's Church the parish church of Newhaven.

Courtesy of Newhaven Museum

On 14th October 1891, Rose Banks of Seaford was due to marry Henry N Wood junior of Newhaven. This young couple had apparently been engaged for seven years and during this time they had been saving up to buy a home of their own. Mr Wood was a second engineer on the cross channel ferry, earning £190 a year. As he lived with his parents, he had been able to save some of his money. Finally, the young couple took a house in Newhaven and, on the 26th September, Mr Wood went to Mr Buck, the clergyman from Seaford, to have the Banns published. The marriage was arranged for the 14th October.

All appeared to be going well. The guests arrived, some from a distance, ready for the ceremony to commence at one o'clock. One o'clock then one thirty passed as did two and three o'clock without any bridegroom appearing. In the end, the disappointed bride and guests returned to the house where the wedding breakfast had been prepared. All the bride and guests could do was to console themselves with the breakfast. Mr Wood's father arrived and feared that his son had drowned in a stream to which, in court, Mr Marshall Hall responded that the stream "must have been one of whisky".

The Groom was later found by the bride's brother in the waiting room of the railway station at Brighton. Before he could give an explanation to his future brother in law, it was reported that he held Henry's nose and boxed his ears, which brought laughter to the court. At that point Henry had run off and disappeared.

The reason for the court case was that Rose's mother, a widow who possessed a fair income, had lent £9 to Mr Wood for a ring. This money had not been returned as promised. Rose also had an expensive trousseau provided by her mother which cost £50 and 60 guests had been invited. The jury awarded Rose Banks damages of £275.[103]

≈≈≈≈≈≈≈≈≈

1896.

Nothing is new and this crime shows that greed has always affected those who have access to money. The first reports of this robbery appeared on Sunday night 13th September 1896 and it did seemed like it was what could be termed as, a normal robbery. Barclays Bank in Newhaven, formerly a branch of Molineaux, Whitfield & Co's bank, had been broken into, with the manager tied up and found unconscious. A reward of £100 was offered, as over £1000 had been stolen. In the early reports, the public were told that two men had been involved in the robbery. To help find the supposed robbers, a local shopkeeper had identified a pocket-knife that was left behind at the bank as being the same bought by a strange man a week earlier.

Details of the robbery were to take a strange turn within a few days of the crime being reported. At the end of the week it was sensationally announced that Superintendent Stephens and Sergeant Willard of the local constabulary had arrested, Mr Kennard the manager of the bank and a highly respected member of the community.

The subsequent court cases were initially held in the police court and then in the assize and quickly show that this was not a robbery with violence, but a possible way of hiding serious fraud. On the day of the alleged robbery, Dr Cann, the local Newhaven surgeon, attended the bank to check on the injuries of Mr Kennard In court, Dr Cann agreed that the injuries could have been self-inflected and, therefore, it was possible the prisoner had taken some drug which rendered him unconscious. A locksmith was also called in and he showed that the lock on the front door to the bank could not have been picked. Now it was clear that this was an inside job and not a robbery.

On the left at the corner of Bridge Street and High Street, NatWest Bank formerly London & Counties while past the White Hart would have been Barclays Bank.

Courtesy of Newhaven Museum

Further enquires followed and the story came out that this was the only way the bank manager could think of to get out of his financial troubles. William Kennard had started to speculate in the stock market. Not only had he lost £135 borrowed from his father, but also his wife's money and before using his bank's money to fund his debts. To cover his losses he had taken £400 from the bank. This was quickly ascertained by the police as they made their enquiries. William's problems had become serious a few months earlier and, suddenly, time was running out.

On the 1st July, the Old Bank of Molineaux, Whitfield & Co was taken over by Barclay & Co, which meant that, to facilitate a smooth takeover, a check was to be carried out of the assents of each branch. A letter came from Lewes stating that Mr Whitfield, one of the bank's directors, would come to Newhaven on the 30th June to check that the books were in order.

William panicked. He was short of funds, what was he to do? The simple answer was a short term loan from another bank. Newhaven had another bank in the town, a branch of the London and County Bank (now known as NatWest). Nothing seemed strange when William visited his friend, Mr Stone, the manager of the London and County Bank, and asked if he could borrow £400. The explanation was that a client was due the next day and he did not have sufficient cash. Immediately after the visit by the bank's director, the £400 in gold was returned. Not surprisingly, this transaction did not appear in William's books which were, of course, now in order.

William was a well-respected member of the Molineaux bank, having been employed by them for twenty four years. He had recently been promoted to manager of the Newhaven branch at £230 a year along with a rent free house for his wife and family of five children. However, the opportunity of making even more was too big and so he started speculating and used whatever money he could borrow. In all, to cover his stock market losses, he had borrowed £1042 from the bank and his family.

He was very lucky that he had a previous good record, meaning he had to serve a sentence of only five years imprisonment.[104]

References

1 "flotsam and jetsum", Hastings and St Leonards Observer. 18 June 1879. P 6.
2 Online Historical Population Reports.< http://www.histpop.org/ohpr/servlet/Show?page=Home> [accessed 29 August 2011]
3 'The New Harbour Works at Newhaven', *The Morning Post* (London) 27 December 1881. P. 3.
4 'Newhaven', in *Pigot and Co's National, London and Provincial Commercial Directory*, (London & Manchester: Pigot & Co, 1831 & 1839)
5 'Newhaven', in *Post Office Directory of Essex, Herts, Middlesex, Kent, Surrey & Sussex*, (London: Kelly & Co, 1845).
6 'Newhaven', in *Post Office Directory of Essex, Herts, Middlesex, Kent, Surrey & Sussex*, (London: Kelly & Co, 1855)
7 *London Gazette*, 22 February 1839. P. 388.
8 "Newhaven: Past and Present" Newhaven and Seaford Magazine December 1864
9 1841 Newhaven Census, <http://www.ancestry.co.uk> [accessed 1 September 2011]
10 see. Women, Business, and Finance in Nineteenth-Century Europe: Rethinking Separate Spheres, ed Robert Beachy, Béatrice Craig, Alastair Owens
11 "Deaths". Sussex Advertiser 16 November 1864 p3.
12 'Newhaven', in Pigot and Co's National, London and Provincial Commercial Directory, (London & Manchester: Pigot & Co, 1831)
13 Marie Dessauer, 'Unemployment Records, 1848-59', *The Economic History Review*, 10 (1940),
14 ESRO, G7-14-1
15 M J Burchall, 'Eastern Sussex workhouse census 1851', Sussex Family History Group Publication. 1978
16 *James Bowker, 'A Corner of Sussex', The Irish Monthly, 17 (1889), p. 642.*
17 The Morning Post, 24 January 1889 p 6
18 *E. V, Lucas, Highways and Byways in Sussex (London: Macmillan & Co. Ltd, 1904), p. 260.*
19 Charles C. B. Dickens, 'Old towns by the sea', All the Year Round, 17 (1876), p. 135.
20 'ART. II.--1. Sussex Archaeological Collections, 1846-1861', *The Quarterly Review*, 112 (1862), P. 70
21 Percy Fitzgerald, 'Holiday Ports', *Belgravia : a London magazine*. 4 (1874), p. 259.
22 "Sale by auction Newhaven Sussex" Sussex Advertiser. 3 February 1840. P2
23 "Newhaven to be sold at auction" Sussex advertiser. 26 June 1820. P1
24 "Newhaven Sussex-valuable freehold property". Sussex Advertiser. 22 August 1865. P8

25 "Freeholds – Newhaven Sussex". Sussex Advertiser. 19 May 1866. P1
26 Gibbs, D. F., 'The Rise of the Port of Newhaven, 1850-1914', *Transport History*, 3 (1970). P260
27 ESRO, HIL 6/61/1 : ESRO, ACC 4954/381 ; ESRO, TD/E/113
28 ESRO, TD/E/113
29 ESRO, TD/E/131
30 ESRO, R/C/4/486/13
31 ESRO R/C/4/22
32 ESRO R/C/4/22
33 ESRO NMB/2/1/3
34 ESRO, HIL-6-61
35 Gregory Clark, *'Land Hunger: Land as a Commodity and as a Status Good, England, 1500-1910', Explorations in Economic History, 35 (1998), p. 60*
36 ESRO ACC 8745/81 (this is a large complex bundle of documents)
37 ESRO ACC 4954/384
38 Sussex Advertiser 1 May 1966 P4 & 26 June 1866 P4.
39 1881 Newhaven Census, <http://www.ancestry.co.uk> [accessed 1 September 2011]
40 Gibbs, D. F., 'The Rise of the Port of Newhaven, 1850-1914', *Transport History*, 3 (1970), 258
41 *Hampshire Telegraph and Sussex Chronicle etc.*, (Portsmouth) 22 March 1851, p. 1.
42 "Newhaven" Sussex Advertiser. 26 September 1865. P6
43 *The Era* (London) 10 December 1865, p. 6. ; *The Era* (London) 19 June 19 1886, p. 20.
44 "To builders", Hastings and St Leonards Observer, 10 July1880 p4
45 According to an Ancesty.co.uk, Emma Towner's husband, Charles, was recorded in the 1881 census as being an inmate at Haywards Heath lunatic asylum and died there two years later.
46 "Newhaven – Extension of oyster culture" The Kent and Sussex Courier 27 June 1877 p3.
47 *The Standard*, (London) 23 March 1871 p 8 (The advertisement shows that this fee paying school was called Albert School)
48 "Newhaven: Past and Present" Newhaven and Seaford Magazine December 1864
49 The Brighton Patriot, 3 July p3 ; and 26 June 1838 p3 ; Sussex Advertiser 2 July 1838 P3
50 TNA: MH 12-13046
51 "Newhaven", Sussex Advertiser. 17 February 1840. P3
52 'Newhaven' Sussex Advertiser 17 May 1890 p3
53 'Newhaven' Sussex Advertiser 15 November 1891 p3
54 'Newhaven' Sussex Advertiser 11 May 1864 p3
55 Newhaven and Seaford magazine April 1864
56 The Ocean – salvage, The Hull Packet (Hull England) Friday 22 June 1838
57 An inquest - The Times 14 September 1838 P7

58 John Bull (London England) Sunday 2 December 1838 p 574
59 The Times 11 October 1841 p7
60 "Sussex coast Loss of Life" The Morning Post, 14 January 1843 P3
61 The Lady's Newspaper (London England) 15 May 1847 p 472
62 "Great storm on the coast" The Morning Chronicle London 27 October 27 1859
63 "Great storm and gale.– two wrecks off Newhaven". The Hampshire Advertiser 25 October 1862 p. 4.
64 Sussex Advertiser 27 January 1800. P3
65 http://www.newhavenlifeboat.co.uk/station.html [accessed 1 April 2013]
66 "rescue of four men" Reynolds Weekly Newspaper, 9 February 1851. P3 ; "Newhaven" Sussex Advertiser, 11 March 1851. P6
67 Newhaven Harbour and Ouse Lower Navigation, Sussex Express 21 October 1851 p5
68 A Souvenir book to commemorate the naming of the Newhaven Lifeboat David & Elizabeth Acland. Paths Publishing (Peacehaven, Sussex) 2000. Tony Payne and Michael Tubb.
69 "The Saving of Life at Sea", The Jewish Chronicle. 21 May 1875, p125
70 "Launch of the 'Michael Henry' Lifeboat at Newhaven, The Jewish Chronicle 7 September 1877. P 7
71 "Launch of the Michael Henry, Life-boat". The Standard (London) 4 September 1877 p 6
72 "The Michael Henry Lifeboat – Jewish children's gift". Daily News (London) 10 March 1898 P7
73 Illustrated London News 11 March 1848 p 166
74 "Another narrative of the escape of Louis Philippe", Sussex Advertiser, 21 March 1848. P3
75 Sussex Advertiser, 16 November 1847. P6 and 7 December 1847 P6.
76 "The bridge riot at Newhaven". Sussex Advertiser 21 January 1851 P5.
77 http://en.wikipedia.org/wiki/Rebeccaites
78 "The bridge riot at Newhaven". Sussex Advertiser 28 January 1851 P5.
79 "Evasion of the toll at Newhaven Bridge". Sussex Advertiser 1 February 1851. P5
80 Sussex Navvies, *Lloyd's Weekly Newspaper,* (London) 21 October 1866, p. 12 ; "The recent affray between the police and the Navvies at Newhaven" Sussex Advertiser 5 September 1866 p3 also see page 2 Another riot between English and Belgian Navvies.
81 Newhaven, Sussex Advertiser 14 July 1866 p2
82 Newhaven, Sussex Advertiser 1 August 1866 p4
83 "Serious conflict between the police and some Navvies at Newhaven". Sussex Advertiser 29 August 1866. p3; "The Recent affray between the police and the Navvies", Sussex Advertiser 5 September 1866 p3
84 "The Naval and Military Riots at Newhaven", Hastings and St Leonards Observer. 13 May 1876 P3 : The Sheffield & Rotherham Independent (Sheffield) 11 May 1876 p 8 : Lloyd's Weekly Newspaper (London) 14 May 1876 soldiers fight in pub

85 Emily Detmer, "Civilizing Subordination: Domestic Violence and The Taming of the Shrew" Shakespeare Quarterly, Vol. 48, No. 3 (Autumn, 1997), pp. 273-294

86 "Murder of a Wife by her husband" The Times 12 Oct 1830 p 4: The Morning Post (London England) 16 October 1830: Hampshire Advertiser 16 October 1830

87 Lewes, Dec. 24. -The Standard (London) 25 December 1830 P4: Winter Assizes Lewes, Friday, 24 Dec, The Times 25 December 1830 p 4

88 Barry Godfrey and Paul Lawrence, "Crime and justice 1750-1950". (Cullompton: Willan Publishing) 2005

89 "The Alleged Murder near Lewes," The Morning Post (London) 20 August 1881 p 6 ; "Alleged Murder", The Times 20 August 1881 p 10 ; "Charge of murder in Sussex", Berrow's Worcester Journal (Worcester) 27 August 1881 p 2 ; "Alleged double murder near Lewes", The Illustrated Police News (London) 27 August 1881 p 2 ; "The Assizes" The Times 4 November 1881 p 11 ; "Assize Intelligence" Daily News (London) 4 November 1881 P2 ; "Assize News" The Standard (London) 4 November 1881 p 3

90 "Murder on the Downs" Lloyd's Weekly Newspaper (London) 9 April 1893 P2 ; "Murdered and Mutilated" The Hampshire Advertiser (Southampton) 12 April 1893 p 1 ; "The Newhaven Tragedy" The Daily News (London) 13 April 1893 p3 ; "Murdered on the South Downs" Illustrated Police News 15 April 1893 p 3 ; "The Newhaven Horror" The Illustrated Police News 22 April 1893 p2 : "Newhaven Murder" The Illustrated Police News etc (London England) Saturday August 19 1893 p3.

91 "Newhaven", The Brighton Patriot. 12 February 1839. P 3 ; "Newhaven", Sussex Advertiser. 11 February 1839 p2

92 "Magistrates' Meeting" Sussex Advertiser. 20 March 1855. P5

93 "A Troublesome Wife" Sussex Advertsiser. 17 July 1855 P4

94 Sussex Advertiser, 21 August 1855. P5

95 "Stealing a ham at Denton". Sussex Advertiser 11 March 1856 P2

96 "Lewes – Summer Assizes" Sussex Advertiser. 24 June 1856. P5

97 "Charge of theft", --The Standard (London England) 6 August 1862 p 6

98 "Charge of Stabbing at Newhaven" Sussex Advertiser, 28 May 1864. P 3 : "Assault at Newhaven", Sussex Advertiser, 5 July 1864. P 7.

99 "An elopement in low life" Dover Express & Kent Intelligence 10 February 1866 P4. : "An elopement in humble life" Sussex Advertiser, 6 February 1866. P5.

100 'Newhaven'. Sussex Advertiser, 20 April 1878 p 3

101 Albert Brookerxe "Albert Brooker", Birmingham Daily Post (Birmingham England) 1 January 1879 P7: Charge of forgery against a relieving Officer, Daily News (London England) 21 January 1879 P6

102 The Sheffield & Rotherham Independent (Sheffield) 10 October 1890 p 4

103 "Missing bridegroom" Lloyd's Weekly Newspaper (London) 13 December 1891 ; "Breach of promise of marriage" Birmingham Daily Post (Birmingham) 8 December 1891 P5 ; "Breach of promise of marriage"The Standard (London) 8 December 1891 p 2

[104] "Bank Robbery" The Huddersfield Daily Chronicle (West Yorkshire) 15 September 1896 p 3 ; "The Newhaven Bank Robbery" The Pall Mall Gazette (London) 17 September 1896 P8 ; The Standard (London) 17 September 1896 p 3 ; "The Newhaven Bank Robbery" The Huddersfield Daily Chronicle (West Yorkshire) 21 September 1896 p 4 ; "The Newhaven Bank Mystery" The Pall Mall Gazette (London) 26 September 1896 P6 ; "The Newhaven Bank Case" The Standard (London) 26 September 1896 p 3 ; "The Bank Robbery" The Illustrated Police News etc (London) September 26 1896 p 6. ; "The Newhaven Bank Case" The Standard (London) 2 October 1896 p 2. ; "The Newhaven Bank Mystery" The Illustrated Police News etc (London) 10 October 1896 p3. ; The Standard (London) 1 December 1896 p 5. ; "A Bank Manager gets five years for a sham burglary" The Illustrated Police News etc (London) 5 December 1896 P 3.

Selected Bibliography

'Abstract of the Evidence on the South-Eastern Brighton, Lewes and Newhaven Railway.', *Bristol Selected Pamphlets*, (1837)
'ART. II.--1. Sussex Archaeological Collections, 1846-1861', *The Quarterly Review*, 112 (1862), 39-82.
Alexander, W. J., 'Speech for the South-Eastern Brighton, Lewes and Newhaven Railway: April 7th, 1837', *Bristol Selected Pamphlets*, (1837)
Andrews, J. H., 'The Development of the Passenger Ports of South-East England', *Geography*, 35 (1950), 239-243
Bailey, Peter S., *Newhaven in Old Picture Postcards*, 1-5 vols (Zaltbommel Netherlands: European library, 1989)
Banister, Fred D., *A Modern History of Newhaven Harbour, with Proposals for its Improvement* (London: Letts, Son & Co, 1879)
Bernard, Stanley. "How did urban population growth in Newhaven (Sussex) affect employment structure, commerce and trade during the period 1837 to 1887" Dissertation submitted for degree of MA (Open University 2012)
Black, Adam and Charles Black, *Black's Guide to Brighton and Vicinity, Including Lewes, Shoreham and Newhaven.*, 9th edn (Edinburgh: A & C Black, 1885)
Borsay, Peter. *The English Urban Renaissance: Culture and Society in the Provincial Town, 1660-1770* (Oxford: Clarendon Press, 1989)
Bowker, James, 'A Corner of Sussex', *The Irish Monthly*, 17 (1889), 641-646
Brandon, P. F., 'The Origin of Newhaven and the Drainage of the Lewes and Laughton Levels', *Sussex Archaeological Collections*, 109 (1971), 95-106
Brent, Colin, *A Short Economic and Social History of Brighton, Lewes and the Downland Region between the Adur and the Ouse, 1500-1900* (Lewes: East Sussex County Council, 1979)
Bridge Group of Companies, *A History of the Newhaven Bridge, 1784-1974 : A Commemorative Book in Aid of the Newhaven Lifeboat and Searchlight Workshops* (Newhaven : Bridge Press, 1974)
'Brighton, Lewes, and Hastings Railway.', *LSE Selected Pamphlets*, (1844)
Broad, John. 'Housing the Rural Poor in Southern England, 1650-1850', *Agricultural History Review*, 48 (2000), 151-70
Brookfield, H. C., *A Regional Study of Urban Development in Coastal Sussex since the Eighteenth Century*, Thesis submitted for the degree of Ph.D, (London School of Economics and Political Science, 1950)
Brookfield, H. C., 'Three Sussex Ports, 1850-1950', *Journal of Transport History*, 2 (1955), 35-50
Carey, A. E., 'Harbour Improvements at Newhaven, Sussex. (Includes Plates and Appendices).', *Minutes of the Proceedings*, 87 (1887), 92-113
Farrant, John H., 'The Harbours of Sussex as Part of an Inland Transport System the Eighteenth and Nineteenth Century', *Sussex Industrial History*, 15 (1985/86), 2-11
Farrant, S. P., 'The Changing Structure of Land Ownership in the Lower Ouse Valley, 1780 to 1840', *Sussex Archaeological Collections*, 116 (1978), 261-267
Farrant, Sue. 'The Management of Four Estates in the Lower Ouse Valley (Sussex) and Agricultural Change, 1840-1920', *Southern History*, 1 (1979), 155-170

Farrant, Sue, 'London by the Sea: Resort Development on the South Coast of England 1880-1939', *Journal of Contemporary History,* 22 (1987), 137-162

Fuller, G. J., 'The Development of Roads in the Surrey. Sussex Weald and Coastlands between 1700 and 1900', *Transactions and Papers (Institute of British Geographers),* (1953), 37-49

Gibbs, D. F., 'The Rise of the Port of Newhaven, 1850-1914', *Transport History,* 3 (1970), 258-82

Godfrey, Barry and Lawrence Paul., "Crime and Justice 1750-1950", (Cullompton Devon: Willan Publishing, 2005)

Horsfield, Thomas W., *The History, Antiquities and Topography of the County of Sussex,* Facsimile reprint 1974, 1 vols (Dorking, Surrey : Kohler and Coombes, 1835)

Hudson, Pat. *The Industrial Revolution* (London: Hodder Arnold, 2005)

Lowerson, John, *Victorian and Edwardian Seaford : An Embryonic Brighton?* (University of Sussex. Centre for Continuing Education, 1975) Lucas, E. V., *Highways and Byways in Sussex* (London: Macmillan & Co. Ltd, 1904)

Margary, Ivan D., 'The Development of Turnpike Roads in Sussex', *Sussex Notes & Queries,* 13:3 (1950), 49-53

Newhaven and Seaford Magazine, 1-12 (1864)

Payne, Tony. *Newhaven in Old Picture Postcards: Lifeboats-Wrecks-Rescues* (Zaltbommel, Netherlands: European Library, 1991)

Salzman, L. F. (ed). 'Parishes: Newhaven.', in *The Victoria History of the Counties of England Sussex,* Volume 7: The rape of Lewes (London: Dawson of Pall Mall, 1940), 62-3

Tate, W. E., *A Handlist of Sussex Inclosure Acts and Awards* (Lewes, Sussex: East Sussex County Council, 1950)

Walker, James. 'Newhaven Harbour, Sussex: Mr Walker's Second Report : 20th June, 1846.', *Hume Tracts,* (1846)

INDEX

Aaron Elphick, 44
Albert King, 30
Alexander Woolgar, 53, 54
Alfred Goldey, 71
Ann Stone, 8
Ark Inn, 29, 43
Benjamin Stace, 74
Bishopstone, 18, 40, 41, 48, 51
Bridge Hotel, 28, 29, 49, 59, 66, 68
Brighton Road, 21, 22, 23, 68
Captain Cheeseman, 40
Caroline Catt, 18
Chapel Road, 16
Charles Brown, 55
Charles Dickens, 12, 33
Charles Stone, 29
Charles Verrall, 60
Charles Woolgar, 30
Coast Guard, 8, 38, 76
Court House Farm, 30
Cyrus Legge, 11
Dr Cann, 82
Earl of Chichester, 15
East View Cottages, 18
Edward Adams, 50, 51
Edward Geering, 53
Elizabeth King, 25
Elizabeth Vigar, 9
Elphick Road, 23, 29
Emily Twiggs, 66
Engineers Arms, 77
Flying Fish, 70, 71, 72
George Akehurst, 64
George Climpson, 55
George Kemp, 25
George Reed, 78
George Smith, 6, 7
George Winter, 58
Heighton, 53
Henry Pettitt, 57
Henry Webber, 71
Holmes Field, 23
Jack Reeves, 7
James Berry, 64
James Diplock, 63, 64, 66
James Lower, 18

Albert Brooker, 79
Alexander Winder, 77
Alexandra Theatre, 28
Ann Dyer, 60, 62
Ann Winter, 60, 63
Bearshide, 28, 42
Benjamin Woolgar, 53
Blue Anchor, 28, 55, 57, 58
Bridge Inn, 6, 8, 9, 16, 29, 34, 35, 36, 48, 50, 51, 60, 61
Canter Hill, 71
Captain Jones, 46
Catt & Sons, 44
Chapel Street, 20, 29, 67
Charles Cooke, 44
Charles Roberts, 41
Charles Trow, 29
Charles William Towner, 6
Clifton Terrace, 18
Cole and Catt, 6, 36
Cricket Ground, 33
Denton Terrace, 18
Dr Noakes, 78
Earl of Sheffield, 15, 33
Edmond Baker, 30
Edward Eager, 58
Elizabeth Akehurst, 64, 65
Elizabeth Winder, 47
Ellen Dooley, 74
Emily Diplock, 63, 64, 65
Emma Towner, 30
Essex Square, 29
Friars Bay, 42, 44
George Brooker, 30
George Cook, 40
George Lower, 75
George Smart, 44
George Stone, 35
Harry Winter, 59, 60, 61, 62
Henry N Wood, 80
Henry Richardson, 57
High Street Miss Catt Cottages, 28
Hope Inn, 29, 69
James Bannister, 30
James Bryant, 57
James Ling, 79
James Simmons, 75

James Washington, 62
Job Taylor, 71
John Bissett, 60
John Camp, 7
John Gray, 9, 26
John Jeffries, 57
John Noakes, 6
John Saunders, 71
John Welch, 51
John Wingfield, 26
Joseph Lower, 42
Lewes Road, 14, 21, 23
Lodge Farm, 64
Louis-Philippe, 47, 48, 49
Mark Woolgar, 30
Mary Ann Stace, 74
Meeching Road, 17, 20, 31, 32, 57, 68
Mr Bishop, 71
Mr Catt, 40, 48, 73
Mr Dorman, 43
Mr Gell, 60
Mr Irons, 49
Mr Muggridge, 73
Mr Soap, 56
Mr T R Scott, 28
Mr Vandenburg, 76
Mrs Stone, 60
Mrs William (Lydia) Adam, 8
PC Moore, 56
PC Osborne, 55, 56
PC Whapham, 58
Philip Mantle, 42
Police Sergeant Renville, 57
Queen Victoria, 1, 2, 13, 33, 35, 46, 49
Richard Belton, 77, 78
Richard Hoare, 76, 77
Royal Oak, 64
Sarah Deane, 10
Sarah Lower, 60, 61
Sarah Tubb, 8, 9
Sergeant Akehurst, 53
Sergeant Willard, 82
Shipyard, 21, 25, 26, 53, 60
Simpson Lower, 17, 23
South Eastern Terrace, 16
St Luke's Lane, 13, 19
Stephen Tucknott, 53

James Woolgar, 29
John Bennett Lee, 16, 17
John Bull, 42
John Carter, 44
John Hubard, 6
John Manser, 57
John Pendrill, 51
John Shepherd, 42
John Wilson, 58
Jolly Sailor, 71
Knowles Field, 50
Lieutenant Franklin, 38
London and Paris Hotel, 12, 28, 29, 31, 46
Major Anderson, 58
Mary Job, 71, 72
Mary Hope, 75, 76
Michael Henry, 45, 46
Mr & Mrs Bond, 18
Mr Brooker, 33
Mr Cole, 38, 48
Mr Duly, 8
Mr Gray, 25
Mr Kemp, 9
Mr Potts, 71
Mr Stevens, 16
Mr Towner, 53
Mrs Reed, 78, 79
Mrs Susannah Gray, 76
Nicholas Massey, 39
PC Osbon, 78
PC Peerless, 74, 75, 76
Peacehaven, 38, 42
Piddinghoe, 16, 63, 64, 70
Portabello, 39, 42
R Towner, 33
Railway Inn, 71, 75
Richard Gantling, 76
Rose Banks, 80, 81
Samuel Worsley, 51
Sarah Dyer, 60
Sarah Smith, 6, 9, 35, 36, 48, 49
Sebag Montefiore, 46
Sergeant Peacock, 56
Ship Inn/Hotel, 28, 29, 61
Shoreham, 24, 40, 64
Sleepers Hole, 44
St John's Place, 14
Stephen Adams, 65
Superintendent Flanagan, 53